Book B

LANGUAGE
Power

gagelearning

Copyright © 1997 Gage Learning Corporation

1120 Birchmount Road, Toronto, Ontario M1K 5G4 1-800-668-0671

www.nelson.com

Adapted from material developed, designed, and copyrighted by Steck-Vaughn.

Editorial Team: Chelsea Donaldson, Carol Waldock
Cover Adaptation: Christine Dandurand

ISBN-13: **978-0-7715-1014-4**
ISBN-10: **0-7715-1014-4**

6 7 8 9 WC 09 08 07 06
Printed and bound in Canada

Table of Contents

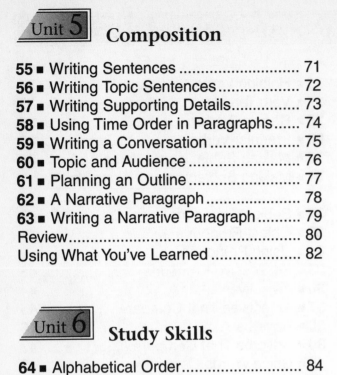

Unit 5 — Composition

Unit 6 — Study Skills

Final Reviews

Lesson 1

Synonyms

> ■ A **synonym** is a word that has the same or almost the same meaning as another word.
>
> EXAMPLES: last – final; leave – go; prize – award

A. For each underlined word, circle its synonym at the end of the sentence.

1. My goal is to become a biologist. (thought, desire)
2. I like going out into the field to study. (outdoors, lab)
3. The best learning comes through observing things in nature. (seeing, changing)
4. I record my findings in a journal. (write, tape)
5. Then I compare what I have seen with what books say. (question, match)
6. If there is a difference, I consult my teacher. (direct, ask)
7. Together we explore possible theories. (ideas, facts)
8. Sometimes there are only small differences between theories. (little, large)
9. I like studying plants the most. (enjoy, hate)
10. I raised some bean plants for an experiment. (grew, bought)
11. The experiment worked exactly as planned. (arranged, found)

B. Rewrite these sentences. Use synonyms from the box below for the underlined words.

active	brave	common	glad
halt	large	stay	uncommon

1. The ordinary hive has many worker bees.

   _____

2. It is not unusual to find 80 000 busy workers in a colony.

   _____

3. The fearless worker bee will do anything to stop the enemies of the hive.

   _____

4. The hive must remain warm, or the bees will die.

   _____

5. Farmers are happy to see big hives near their fields.

   _____

Antonyms

> ■ An **antonym** is a word that has the opposite meaning of another word.   EXAMPLES: stop – go; yes – no; hot – cold

A. For each underlined word, write an antonym from the box.

1. <u>dull</u> knife   _____ knife

2. <u>hard</u> cheese   _____ cheese

3. <u>correct</u> answer   _____ answer

4. <u>spend</u> money   _____ money

5. <u>remember</u> groceries   _____ groceries

6. <u>neat</u> room   _____ room

7. <u>finish</u> chores   _____ chores

8. <u>old</u> clothes   _____ clothes

9. <u>bottom</u> line   _____ line

begin
forget
messy
new
save
sharp
soft
top
wrong

B. Rewrite the paragraph using an antonym for each underlined word.

    The <u>little</u> game was that evening. Scott and Jeff wanted to wear <u>dirty</u> uniforms. They believed that looking <u>bad</u> to the other team would help them win. They <u>dirtied</u> their uniforms at the same time. They used bleach to fade the colours. When they finished <u>wetting</u> the uniforms, they discovered they had been <u>right</u>. Their uniforms were now the <u>opposite</u> colour as those of the other team!

_____

_____

_____

_____

_____

_____

_____

_____

Lesson 3

Homonyms

> ■ A **homonym** is a word that sounds like another word.
> However, it has a different meaning and is spelled differently.
> EXAMPLES: it's, its   their, there, and they're
> It's means "it is." **It's** a nice day.
> Its means "belonging to it." The dog hurt **its** leg.
>
> Their means "belonging to them." That is **their** house.
> There means "in or at that place." Put it **there**.
> They're means "they are." **They're** going to the game.

A. Write it's or its to complete each sentence.

1. The team starts _____ practice at noon.

2. The coach says _____ necessary to practise.

3. I don't believe the players think _____ fun to practise.

4. Others say _____ exciting to watch the game from the sidelines.

5. The team is proud of _____ record.

6. If the team does _____ job, it will win.

7. I think _____ still a month until the championship game.

8. The team thinks _____ chance for winning the championship is good.

9. However, _____ too early to know for sure.

B. Circle the correct homonym in each sentence.

1. (There, Their, They're) is no reason to believe something is wrong.

2. (There, Their, They're) only a few minutes late.

3. I'm sure (there, their, they're) fine and will be here soon.

4. You know (there, their, they're) habits.

5. Wherever they go, they get (there, their, they're) late.

6. (There, Their, They're) families are like that, too.

7. I don't understand why (there, their, they're) always late.

8. Maybe (there, their, they're) clocks are wrong!

Lesson 4

More Homonyms

> ■ Remember that a **homonym** is a word that sounds like another
> word.   EXAMPLES: to, two, too   right, write   hear, here
>
> To means "toward" or "to do something." Go **to** the store.
> Two means "the number 2." Buy **two** litres of milk.
> Too means "also" or "more than enough." It's **too** hot.
>
> Write means "to put words or numbers onto paper."
> Did you **write** the letter?
> Right means "correct" or "the opposite of left."
> Turn **right** at the corner.
>
> Hear means "listen." Didn't you **hear** me?
> Here means "in this place." Meet me **here** in one hour.

A. Write to, two, or too to complete each sentence.

1. It was _____ years ago that José and I went on
   vacation _____ the mountains.

2. We thought about going back last year, _____ , but we
   decided not _____ .

3. We both thought going _____ the beach would be more fun.

4. Since only _____ of us were going, we thought we'd meet more
   people there.

B. Write right or write to complete each sentence.

1. I'll _____ directions for finding my house.

2. You'll need a map to find the _____ roads.

3. Go ten kilometres and turn _____ at the bridge.

4. You're on the _____ road if you pass the mall.

C. Write hear or here to complete each sentence.

1. "I can't _____ you because of the music," shouted Alan.

2. "Come _____ so I can _____ you better," said Peter.

3. "Why did we come _____ to talk? I can't _____ anything," said Alan.

4. "Let's get out of _____ ," said Peter.

Multiple Meanings

> ■ Some words have more than one meaning. They are spelled the same, and often are pronounced the same, but they mean different things. The only way to know the meaning of these words is to see how they are used in a sentence.
>
> EXAMPLES: I **can** go.   Get the **can** of beans.

A. Circle the correct meaning for each underlined word.

1. She put the <u>pad</u> behind her back and leaned against it.
   pillow   walk softly

2. A <u>tear</u> rolled down her cheek.
   rip or pull apart   salty liquid from the eye

3. The rain continued to <u>beat</u> against the little cabin.
   strike over and over   to mix

4. As she listened, the warning bell began to <u>ring</u>.
   make the sound of a bell   narrow circle of metal worn on the finger

5. The pounding waves made a terrible <u>racket</u>.
   light bat used in sports   loud noise

6. Her cabin would soon be lost to the <u>storm</u>.
   attack   heavy winds with rain or snow

7. Her only hope was that someone would come and <u>lead</u> her to safety.
   soft metal   guide

B. Write a sentence for each meaning of the words given.

1. <u>wind</u>: blowing air

   _____

   <u>wind</u>: to tighten the spring of

   _____

2. <u>rock</u>: to move back and forth

   _____

   <u>rock</u>: a large stone

   _____

Lesson 6

Prefixes

> ■ A **prefix** is a syllable added to the beginning of a word to change the meaning of the word.
>
> EXAMPLES:
> The prefix dis- means "not" or "the opposite of."   **dis**appear
> The prefix mis- means "bad(ly)" or "wrong(ly)."   **mis**behave
> The prefix re- means "again" or "back."   **re**do
> The prefix un- means "not" or "the opposite of."   **un**friendly

A. Complete each sentence by adding un- or dis- to the word in parentheses.

1. Tabor the Great made a man _____ from the stage.   (appear)

2. The man looked _____ about what would happen to him.   (concerned)

3. He seemed _____ that he was even on the stage.   (aware)

4. The man vanished! The audience tried to _____ where he'd gone. (cover)

5. But the man reappeared and was _____ .   (harmed)

6. It would be hard to _____ an act as great as Tabor's.   (like)

7. No one could _____ with the fact that it had been a fine evening. (agree)

B. Complete each sentence by adding mis- or re- to the word in parentheses.

1. I _____ the plan for the park at the edge of town.   (understood)

2. I didn't want to see a _____ of such fine land.   (use)

3. The plan is to _____ our town as it was long ago.   (create)

4. It will help us to _____ the history of the town.   (live)

5. I really _____ the plan.   (judged)

6. I should learn not to _____ before I know all the facts.   (act)

© 1997 Gage Educational Publishing Company   **Unit 1, Vocabulary**

Lesson 7 — Suffixes

> ■ A **suffix** is a syllable added to the end of a word to change the meaning of the word.
>
> EXAMPLES:
>
> The suffix -**ful** means "full of," "able to," or "the amount that will fill." hope**ful**, help**ful**, spoon**ful**
>
> The suffix -**less** means "without" or "not able to do." hope**less**, harm**less**

A. In each blank, write the word that matches the definition in parentheses.

effortless	worthless	meaningful	endless
successful	careless	joyless	tireless

1. Giving a _____ party is not always easy.   (full of success)

2. When planning a party, I am _____ .   (not able to tire)

3. If the party is well planned, it looks _____ .   (without effort)

4. A _____ mistake can ruin a party.   (without care)

5. A _____ game helps people to get into the spirit of the party.
   (full of meaning)

6. There is an _____ number of party games.   (without end)

7. But all of the planning is _____ if no one comes.
   (without worth)

8. It would be a _____ evening if no one came to my party!
   (without joy)

B. Write a definition for the underlined word in each phrase.

1. <u>colourless</u> soap   _____ without colour _____

2. <u>bottomless</u> pit   _____

3. <u>sorrowful</u> event   _____

4. <u>beautiful</u> car   _____

5. <u>flavourless</u> meal   _____

Compound Words

> ■ A **compound word** is a word formed by putting two or more words together. EXAMPLES: railway, textbook

A. Write the two words that form each underlined compound word.

1. We are planning a picnic this <u>weekend</u>.

   _____   _____

2. Tess is bringing her delicious <u>homemade</u> chicken.

   _____   _____

3. My job is to bring the <u>watermelon</u>.

   _____   _____

4. The picnic will be over at <u>sunset</u>.

   _____   _____

B. Combine words from the box to form compound words. Use a compound word to complete each sentence.

fire   front   watch   speaker   water   boat   place   tug   man   loud

1. The _____ inched slowly into the harbour.

2. Dock workers were waiting on the _____ .

3. Using the _____ , the captain called the crew to the deck.

4. As he waved to Mike, the night _____ , he felt glad to be going home.

5. He would soon be home sitting in front of his warm _____ .

C. Combine the words below to form four compound words. Use each word in a sentence of your own.

news   night   note   base   mid   ball   paper   book

1. _____ _____

2. _____ _____

3. _____ _____

4. _____ _____

> ■ A **contraction** is a word formed by joining two other words. When the two words are joined, a letter or letters are left out. An **apostrophe** (') is used to show where the missing letter or letters would be.
>
> EXAMPLE: I ~~would~~ – I'd   he ~~is~~ – he's   We ~~have~~ – we've
>
> ■ The only contraction that breaks this rule is won't. Won't means "will not." The i̲ becomes o̲ when the other letters are dropped.

A. Rewrite each sentence using a contraction for the words in parentheses.

1. (I will) need volunteers for the newspaper.

   _____

2. The first stories are due soon, so (we have) got to hurry.

   _____

3. (You will) each be given a section of the paper to work on.

   _____

4. Joyce says (she is) looking forward to the first copy.

   _____

5. Anthony says (he is) going to help us.

   _____

B. Underline the contraction in each sentence. Write the two words that make up each contaction.

1. Joe can't play in the hockey game tonight.

   _____   _____

2. He didn't remember to bring his uniform.

   _____   _____

3. The coach won't let him play without a uniform.

   _____   _____

4. Joe isn't happy about missing the game.

   _____   _____

5. No one thinks we'll win without Joe.

   _____   _____

A. Rewrite each sentence using a synonym for each underlined word.

   1. The <u>large</u> dog chewed on the <u>small</u> bone.

_____

   2. He was not <u>frightened</u> by the <u>strange</u> sight.

_____

B. Find the pair of synonyms in each sentence. Write each pair on the lines.

   1. She whispered the whole time, so we missed the entire movie.

     _____   _____

   2. They built the house first, and then constructed the garage.

     _____   _____

C. Rewrite each sentence using an antonym for each underlined word.

   1. The <u>tiny</u> fire is <u>cold</u>. _____

   2. The <u>old</u> joke made me <u>cry</u>. _____

D. For each underlined word, circle the correct antonym at the end of the sentence.

   1. It's hard to believe they could do such a <u>foolish</u> thing.   (wise, funny)

   2. It became a <u>funny</u> story to tell their friend.   (sad, long)

   3. The story did not <u>amuse</u> her, however.   (entertain, sadden)

E. Circle the correct word or words to complete each sentence.

   1. I can (hear, here) the speaker very clearly.

   2. I have (to, too, two) tickets (to, too, two) this event.

   3. (Its, It's) interesting to see the statue on (its, it's) stand.

   4. She asked us to (write, right) our names the (write, right) way.

   5. They expected to find (they're, their) friends already (there, their).

F. Circle the correct meaning of each underlined word.

   1. The <u>wind</u> howled through the valley.

     to coil or turn   moving air

   2. He watched the river <u>wind</u> on its way.

     to coil or turn   moving air

G. Write a sentence for the meaning given for each underlined word.

1. <u>batter</u>: person at bat

   _____

   <u>batter</u>: mixture for cooking

   _____

2. <u>duck</u>: a water bird

   _____

   <u>duck</u>: lower the head

   _____

H. Add <u>mis-</u>, <u>dis-</u>, <u>re-</u>, <u>un-</u>, <u>-ful</u> or <u>-less</u> to the words in parentheses to complete each sentence.

1. I _____ (agree) with _____ (turning) books to the library late.

2. It is _____ (thought) to _____ (use) your right to the books.

3. Be _____ (thank) for _____ (limited) use of the library.

I. Combine words from the box to make compound words. Use the compound words to complete each sentence.

air   cut   door   hair   port   knob

1. We started our trip at the _____ .

2. Richard's reflection told him it was time for a _____ .

3. Jill turned the _____ slowly, and the door creaked open.

J. Underline the contractions in each sentence. Write the two words that make up each contraction.

1. I'd like to try mountain climbing, but I'm too scared.

   _____   _____

2. As long as he's happy, it doesn't matter what job he has.

   _____   _____

3. She didn't know what she'd do next.

   _____   _____

Using What You've Learned

A. Rewrite the paragraph using synonyms for each underlined word.

The little man carried a large suitcase. He seemed to be trying to
locate someone. Suddenly an auto screeched to a halt. The man grinned
when he saw his best friend in the car.

_____

_____

_____

_____

B. Complete the paragraph. Write the correct homonym in each space.

I have no choice. I'll have to stay home until Amanda gets

_____ (here, hear). Irene is _____

(to, too, two) young _____ (to, too, two) be left alone.

_____ (There, They're, Their) is no one else to watch

her. _____ (Its, It's) wrong for you to think I'd leave a

child who's _____ (to, too, two) years old alone. I'll

wait to _____ (here, hear) from Amanda. Until then,

_____ (there, they're, their) just going to have to

get along without me. I know this is the _____

(write, right) thing to do.

C. Read the definitions of each word. Then write one sentence for each meaning given.

1. brush: tool for painting

_____

brush: bushes

_____

2. fly: insect

_____

fly: move through the air with wings

_____

D. Use <u>mis-</u>, <u>dis-</u>, <u>un-</u>, or <u>-ful</u> with one of the underlined words in each sentence to form a new word. Rewrite each sentence using the new word. Be sure the sentence keeps the same meaning.

1. I am <u>not happy</u> with the way the tape sounds.

_____

2. I was <u>full of hope</u> that this tape would be good.

_____

3. Now it seems that I <u>wrongly judged</u> it.

_____

4. I'm still <u>not satisfied</u> with the way it sounds.

_____

E. Combine the words below to form three compound words. Then use each word in a sentence of your own.

| camp | post | light | fire | card | flash |

1. _____

_____

2. _____

_____

3. _____

_____

F. Underline all of the contractions in the paragraph. Then write each contraction and the two words from which it is made.

There isn't much I wouldn't do for my grandmother. She's the most wonderful person I know. I can't imagine not going to her house for Sunday dinner. Everyone in our family enjoys those visits, and we're all glad to have her close by.

1. _____   _____   _____

2. _____   _____   _____

3. _____   _____   _____

4. _____   _____   _____

5. _____   _____   _____

> ■ A **sentence** is a group of words that expresses a complete thought.
>
> EXAMPLES: Ralph washed the car. He drove to the store.

A. Write S on the line if the group of words is a sentence.

_____ **1.** Sarah ran to the car.

_____ **2.** She was in a big hurry.

_____ **3.** All of a sudden.

_____ **4.** Sarah stared at the car.

_____ **5.** She couldn't believe her eyes.

_____ **6.** Three of the tires.

_____ **7.** Were completely flat.

_____ **8.** Sarah had no idea what caused the flats.

_____ **9.** Up the driveway toward the house.

_____ **10.** An open box of nails.

B. Write S on the line if the group of words is a sentence. If it is not a sentence, rewrite it as a sentence by adding whatever is needed.

1. The parents' club has its monthly meeting tonight.

_____

2. All of the parents.

_____

3. A slide show about fire drills will be shown.

_____

4. Following the slide show.

_____

5. The parents will take information home.

_____

Declarative and Interrogative Sentences

- A sentence that makes a statement is called a **declarative sentence**. EXAMPLE: We have two dogs.
- A sentence that asks a question is called an **interrogative sentence**. EXAMPLE: Do you have a dog?

A. Write declarative if the sentence makes a statement. Write interrogative if the sentence asks a question.

_____ **1.** How are you today?

_____ **2.** You didn't look well yesterday.

_____ **3.** I hope you're not getting sick.

_____ **4.** Are you getting enough rest?

_____ **5.** You really can't afford to get sick.

_____ **6.** Isn't the big play this week?

_____ **7.** You need to be healthy for this play.

_____ **8.** Will you be here tomorrow?

_____ **9.** We are going to rehearse before the show.

_____ **10.** Are you ready for the show?

_____ **11.** Did you rehearse much?

_____ **12.** I rehearsed a lot.

_____ **13.** Do you think the practice will help?

_____ **14.** I get so nervous about performing.

_____ **15.** How do you stay so calm?

_____ **16.** Will you help me rehearse?

_____ **17.** I could use some help.

_____ **18.** You're really a good friend.

B. Write one declarative sentence and one interrogative sentence about performing.

1. _____

2. _____

Changing Sentences

> ■ A statement can be made into a question by changing the order of the words in the sentence. EXAMPLE: You are going to the show. Are you going to the show?
> ■ Sometimes a question word like <u>who</u>, <u>why</u>, <u>what</u>, <u>does</u>, or <u>how</u> must also be added to the statement to change it to a question. EXAMPLE: The show is two hours long. How long is the show?

A. Turn each statement into a question by changing the order of the words.

1. I am finished. _____

2. You shouldn't be finished. _____

3. This is taking too long. _____

4. You are leaving. _____

5. You can stay. _____

B. Turn the statements below into questions. You may change the order of the words and add question words as needed.

1. Amina starts her new job today.

   _____

2. She begins at nine o'clock.

   _____

3. She will leave home at eight o'clock.

   _____

4. Amina likes to work on cars.

   _____

5. Repairing cars is very interesting.

   _____

6. Amina is sure she will like this job.

   _____

7. Amina will do a good job.

   _____

- A sentence that gives a command is called an **imperative sentence**.
  EXAMPLES: Sit down. Read your book.
- A sentence that shows surprise or emotion is called an **exclamatory sentence**.
  EXAMPLES: Oh, you scared me! We won the game!

A. Write <u>imperative</u> if the sentence gives a command. Write <u>exclamatory</u> if the sentence shows surprise or emotion.

_____   **1.** You go first, Jack.

_____   **2.** Tell me if it's safe.

_____   **3.** I'm scared!

_____   **4.** Keep your voice down.

_____   **5.** I can't see!

_____   **6.** I'm lost!

_____   **7.** Be quiet.

_____   **8.** Come down here, Pete.

_____   **9.** I'm falling!

_____   **10.** Hurray, I'm out!

_____   **11.** Close the window.

_____   **12.** Watch out for that car.

B. Pretend that you are walking with a friend in a deep, dark forest. Write three imperative sentences and three exclamatory sentences.

1. _____

2. _____

3. _____

4. _____

5. _____

6. _____

Lesson 14

Subjects and Predicates

> ■ Every sentence has two parts. The **subject** of a sentence tells who or what the sentence is about. The **predicate** tells what the subject does or what happens to the subject.
>
> EXAMPLE: The marching band won the championship.
> **Subject** – The marching band; **Predicate** – won the championship

A. Add a subject to each predicate to make a sentence.

1. _____ play tennis.

2. _____ run.

3. _____ returned the ball.

4. _____ won the game.

B. Add a predicate to each subject to make a sentence.

1. Players _____ .

2. Some fans _____ .

3. Coaches _____ .

4. Judges _____ .

C. Write subject or predicate to tell which part of each sentence is underlined.

_____ 1. Tennis is a game.

_____ 2. It is played with a racket.

_____ 3. The player swings the racket.

_____ 4. A ball is also needed.

_____ 5. Two or four players may play at one time.

_____ 6. Love means zero points in tennis.

_____ 7. A set is won in six games.

D. Draw one line under each subject and two lines under each predicate.

1. Tennis was invented by Major Walter Wingfield.

2. The game was called tennis-on-the-lawn.

3. The first Canadian championship took place in 1890.

4. Tennis is a popular game.

5. Patricia Hy is a famous tennis player.

6. You can play tennis, too.

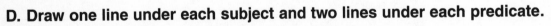

> - The **simple subject** is the main word in the subject part of a sentence. The simple subject is usually a noun or a pronoun.
> - The **simple predicate** is the main word or words in the predicate. The simple predicate is a verb and any helping verbs it may have.
>
>   EXAMPLE: My cousin keeps his car in the garage.
>
>   **Simple Subject** – cousin   **Simple Predicate** – keeps

A. Underline each subject. Then circle each simple subject within each subject.

1. The plans for a new car are made years ahead of time.

2. Many important decisions go into the design of a car.

3. Each part of the car is studied.

4. A clay model is made to show what the car will look like.

B. Underline each predicate. Then circle the simple predicate within each predicate.

1. Seven kinds of bears live in the world.

2. Most bears live in areas north of the equator.

3. Bears have small eyes.

4. Bears can live as long as thirty years.

5. A bear uses its claws to dig for food.

6. Brown bears usually eat grasses, berries, and nuts.

7. Seals and other animals are food for a polar bear.

8. Most bears sleep all winter.

9. Pandas are not really bears at all.

C. Write the simple subject and the simple predicate of each sentence.

1. Modern-day basketball was invented by a Canadian in 1891.

   _____   _____

2. The first Olympic basketball game was in 1936.

   _____   _____

3. Many professional teams play the sport today.

   _____   _____

Lesson 16

Simple and Compound Sentences

> ■ A **simple sentence** has one subject and one predicate.
>   EXAMPLE: Fresh paint brightens a room.
>
> ■ A compound sentence is two simple sentences joined together by words such as and, but, so, and or.
>   EXAMPLE: I painted the den, **and** Kim painted the kitchen.

A. Write simple or compound before each sentence.

_____ 1. We wanted to go on a trip, so we had to make plans.

_____ 2. I voted for Vancouver, but Shanthi voted for the Rocky Mountains.

_____ 3. Shanthi got her way.

_____ 4. Finally, the day to start arrived.

_____ 5. I drove the camper, and Shanthi followed in the car.

_____ 6. The scenery was wonderful.

_____ 7. The Rockies are almost too big to look real.

_____ 8. We wanted to stay in Banff, but it was too crowded.

_____ 9. We could sleep in the open, or we could use a tent.

_____ 10. We decided to use a tent.

B. Make a compound sentence by adding a simple sentence to each group of words below.

1. Sleeping outside is fun, but

_____

2. The Rockies are a great place to visit, and

_____

3. We could pack a lunch, or

_____

4. Hiking looks easy, but

_____

© 1997 Gage Educational Publishing Company

Combining Sentences

- Short sentences about the same subject can often be **combined** into one sentence. Connecting words such as <u>and</u>, <u>but</u>, and <u>or</u> may be used to combine sentences.

  EXAMPLE: Sam went to the store. Joan went to the store, too. They went in a red car. **Combined sentence** – Sam and Joan went to the store in a red car.

A. Combine each pair of sentences.

1. We have to write a report. The report is on history.

   _____

2. My subject is the War of 1812. My subject is Tecumseh.

   _____

3. We must use the encyclopedia. We must use other books.

   _____

4. I should stop wasting time. I should start my report.

   _____

B. Combine each set of sentences into one sentence.

1. Ruben bought a horse. It is big. The horse is brown.

   _____

2. The horse is kept in a barn. The barn is red. The barn is old.

   _____

3. Ruben rides the horse. Lynn rides the horse. They ride in a field.

   _____

C. Write three short sentences about an animal. Then combine your sentences into one sentence.

_____

_____

_____

_____

© 1997 Gage Educational Publishing Company

18 Avoiding Run-on Sentences

■ A **run-on sentence** is two or more sentences that run together without correct punctuation. Correct a run-on sentence by making separate sentences from its parts.

EXAMPLE: Many plants have seeds, the seeds grow into more plants, then those plants have seeds. **Correction** – Many plants have seeds. The seeds grow into more plants. Then those plants have seeds.

■ **Rewrite each story by separating each run-on sentence.**

One morning we found a baby bird it had been knocked from its nest by high winds its mother was nowhere to be seen. It was too young to fly, we took it inside to care for it. We were excited about taking care of the bird, we didn't know what to do about feeding it.

1. _____

2. _____

3. _____

4. _____

5. _____

6. _____

7. _____

The bird's little mouth flew open so often that we could not find enough insects to feed it. Then we found that the little bird liked dog food it also liked little bits of cooked egg yolk we even made some worms out of hamburger meat.

1. _____

2. _____

3. _____

4. _____

A. Write S on the line if the group of words is a sentence. Write X on the line if it is not a sentence.

_____ 1. The first railway across Canada.

_____ 2. The CPR was completed in 1885.

_____ 3. Donald Smith drove in the last spike.

_____ 4. Linked the country from coast to coast.

B. Write interrogative if the sentence is a question. If the sentence is a statement, rewrite it as a question.

1. Talia flew to Montréal. _____

2. Have you ever been to Montréal? _____

3. Did you fly, or did you take the train? _____

4. Taking the train is slower. _____

C. Write imperative if the sentence is a command. Write exclamatory if the sentence shows surprise or emotion.

_____ 1. Be more careful on this test.

_____ 2. Take your time.

_____ 3. Concentrate and read everything well.

_____ 4. I can't believe it!

_____ 5. My score was the highest in the class!

D. Draw one line under the subject and two lines under the predicate of each sentence. Then circle the simple subject and the simple predicate.

1. My cousin Lee plays hockey for the Jets.

2. He practises early every morning.

3. Hockey players love the sport.

4. They play even in the coldest weather.

5. The game of hockey has very dedicated players and fans.

6. Players skate madly around the rink.

E. Write <u>simple</u> if the sentence is a simple sentence. Write <u>compound</u> if the sentence is a compound sentence.

_____ **1.** I went to the movies, and they stayed home.

_____ **2.** I think I had more fun.

_____ **3.** Then they decided to go to the same movie.

_____ **4.** I stayed home, and I still had more fun.

F. Rewrite the run-on sentence as shorter sentences.

Hank got up early he reviewed his notes again, so the test today would be easy for him.

_____

_____

G. Combine the sentences into a single sentence.

Andrea likes chicken. She likes chicken that is baked.

_____

H. Separate each run-on sentence in the paragraph below. Then write each sentence on a line.

I was tired of moving, my family had moved four times in the past three years. Leaving my friends was always the hardest it's not easy to start over and make new ones, now we can stay put in a town that I like.

1. _____

2. _____

3. _____

4. _____

5. _____

I. Write the type of sentence shown in parentheses on each line below.

(interrogative) **1.** _____

(declarative) **2.** _____

(imperative) **3.** _____

(exclamatory) **4.** _____

A. Write <u>sentence</u> on the line if the group of words is a sentence.
If the group of words is not a sentence, rewrite it as a sentence.

1. Lee and Kenji are from Japan._____

2. Three years ago, they._____

3. Now they._____

4. Lee and Kenji like their new home._____

B. Underline the declarative sentences. Write the interrogative sentences.

Can you guess what we call a group of owls? It is called a parliament of owls. What do you think a group of bears is called? Bears gather in a sloth of bears. A gathering of toads is a knot. We also speak of a skulk of foxes and a peep of chickens. I wonder what other group names there are. Do you know any?

1. _____

2. _____

3. _____

C. Rewrite the statements as questions.

1. Jetta ran to the grocery store.

_____

2. She bought bread and milk.

_____

3. She stopped at the park.

_____

4. Jetta was surprised at how long she was gone.

_____

D. Write one imperative sentence and one exclamatory sentence about an adventure.

1. _____

2. _____

E. Draw one line under the subject and two lines under the predicate of each sentence. Then write the simple subject and the simple predicate of each sentence.

Fingerprints can prove who a person is. A light powder is used so fingerprints can be seen. Each person's fingerprints are different from anyone else's fingerprints. Even the fingerprints of twins are different. A person's fingerprints stay the same as he or she grows older.

1. _____   _____

2. _____   _____

3. _____   _____

4. _____   _____

5. _____   _____

F. Underline the compound sentences. Write the simple sentences.

The Magdalen Islands are in the Gulf of St. Lawrence. There are sixteen islands in the group. Lobsters are caught there, and several kinds of fish are also caught. Fishing is the main industry on the islands, but tourism is also important. The capital of the Magdalen Islands is Cap-aux-Meules.

1. _____

2. _____

3. _____

G. Rewrite the paragraph. Combine short sentences and separate run-on sentences.

Flies are interesting insects. The eyes of a fly have up to 400 parts they really see only motion and light. A fly has six legs. Each fly has six feet. Each foot has a pair of claws.

_____

_____

_____

_____

_____

> ■ A noun is a word that names a person, place, or thing.
>   EXAMPLES: person – woman, Anna; place – city, Halifax;
>   thing – dog, Fido

A. Underline the two nouns in each sentence.

1. Mrs. Smith has a big job ahead.
2. She needs to plan a picnic for her family.
3. Mrs. Smith must find a big park.
4. The family always enjoys the picnic.
5. It is a big event every year.
6. Mr. Smith is planning some games.
7. He will set up a net for volleyball.
8. Margie will make the hamburgers.
9. Mrs. Smith finally picked Riverside Park.
10. The park is on the Speed River.

B. Tell what each underlined noun is by writing person, place, or thing.

_____ 1. Buttons the dog

_____ 2. my brother John

_____ 3. the neighbour's uncle

_____ 4. 472 Elm Street

_____ 5. Orville's friend

_____ 6. Morris the cat

_____ 7. the city of Trenton

_____ 8. presented by the mayor

_____ 9. Sydney, Australia

_____ 10. my friend's sister

_____ 11. the province of Québec

_____ 12. a large cloud

_____ 13. a happy clown

Lesson 20

Proper and Common Nouns

> - A **proper noun** names a particular person, place, or thing. It begins with a capital letter.
>   EXAMPLES: person – Mary; place – Truro; thing – Grey Cup
> - A **common noun** does not name a particular person, place, or thing.
>   EXAMPLES: person – girl; place – city; thing – house

A. Underline the common nouns in each sentence.

1. My cousin Monica will visit for the holidays.
2. She loves Thanksgiving in the country.
3. My cousin is always a welcome visitor.
4. Her stories about Calgary are interesting.
5. This year, she is bringing Dr. Alvarado with her.

B. Underline the proper nouns in each sentence.

1. Dr. Alvarado is a doctor in Calgary.
2. She works at the Foothills Hospital.
3. In September, she's going to teach a class in medicine.
4. The class will be at the University of Alberta in Edmonton, Alberta.
5. The students come from all over Canada.

C. Write a proper noun for each common noun given.

1. dog _____Spot_____
2. country _____
3. name _____
4. day _____
5. city _____
6. holiday _____
7. month _____
8. uncle _____
9. cat _____
10. friend _____

11. province _____
12. father _____
13. game _____
14. street _____
15. planet _____
16. school _____
17. teacher _____
18. continent _____
19. prime minister _____
20. magazine _____

 Unit 3, Grammar and Usage

Lesson 21

Singular and Plural Nouns

- A **singular noun** names one person, place, or thing.
- A **plural noun** names more than one person, place, or thing.
- Add -s to most nouns to make them plural.
    - EXAMPLE: dog – dogs
- Add -es to nouns ending in s, z, x, ch, or sh to make them plural.
    - EXAMPLES: dress – dresses, box – boxes
- If a noun ends in a vowel and y, add -s to make it plural. If the noun ends in a consonant and y, change the y to i and add -es.
    - EXAMPLES: bay – bays, party – parties
- If a noun ends with the f sound, change the f to v and add -es.
    - EXAMPLE: calf – calves
- Sometimes the entire spelling is changed to form a plural noun.
    - EXAMPLES: child – children, goose – geese, mouse – mice

A. Write S before each singular noun below. Then write its plural form. Write P before each plural noun. Then write its singular form. You may wish to check the spellings in a dictionary.

_____ 1. porch _____

_____ 2. chair _____

_____ 3. girls _____

_____ 4. wife _____

_____ 5. flies _____

_____ 6. sky _____

_____ 7. foxes _____

_____ 8. halves _____

_____ 9. pencil _____

_____ 10. alley _____

_____ 11. leaves _____

_____ 12. pouch _____

_____ 13. stitches _____

_____ 14. shelf _____

B. Circle the correct noun in parentheses. Write singular or plural on the lines.

_____ 1. After dinner we watch two (program, programs).

_____ 2. We limit our television viewing to one (hour, hours) a day.

_____ 3. The rest of the (time, times), we read or just chat about our day.

_____ 4. Our (family, families) has grown closer since we started this habit.

_____ 5. In fact, Lupe now prefers one of her (magazines, magazine) to TV.

_____ 6. I still like to watch a good (show, shows) now and then.

Lesson 22

Singular Possessive Nouns

- A **possessive noun** is a noun that tells who or what owns something.
- Add an apostrophe (') and an -s to the end of most singular nouns to show that they are possessive nouns.
  EXAMPLES: Tony's house, the dog's bone

A. Rewrite each of the phrases below using a possessive noun.

1. the house of my aunt   my aunt's house

2. the dog my cousin has   _____

3. the books belonging to my friend   _____

4. the bicycle of my brother   _____

5. an apron belonging to the cook   _____

B. Write the correct possessive form of the word in parentheses to complete each sentence.

1. (Jerry) _____ car was stolen.

2. The police (officer) _____ response was not encouraging.

3. He said the (thief) _____ trail was already cold.

4. He reported the (automobile) _____ last location.

5. Jerry hopes his (city) _____ police department will find it.

C. Write the correct possessive noun to complete the second sentence in each pair of sentences.

1. The store is having a sale. The _____ sale will last a week.

2. Lisa bought a coat. _____ coat has a heavy lining.

3. A clerk helped Lisa. The _____ job was to help people.

4. One shopping bag broke. The _____ contents spilled.

5. Another man helped her. Lisa was grateful for the

_____ kindness.

      Unit 3, Grammar and Usage

- A **plural possessive** noun shows ownership by more than one person or thing.
- If a plural noun does not end in -s, the possessive is formed by adding an apostrophe and an -s (**'s**) to the noun.
  EXAMPLE: men's teams
- If a plural noun ends in -s, the possessive is usually formed by simply adding an apostrophe after the -s (**s'**).
  EXAMPLE: birds' nests

A. Write the correct plural possessive form of the word in parentheses to complete each sentence.

1. My (sisters) _____ band is very popular.

2. The (uniforms) _____ colours are beautiful.

3. The band plays for (parents) _____ clubs.

4. The (members) _____ cheering was loud.

5. The (instruments) _____ sounds were perfect.

B. Write the correct possessive noun to complete the second sentence in each pair of sentences.

1. Fred and Carol are farmers. _____ Farmers' _____ work can be very hard.

2. Their children help on the farm. Fred depends on the

   _____ help.

3. There are three ponds on the farm. The _____ water is very clear.

4. Fred keeps many sheep on his farm. He prepares the

   _____ food.

5. He gets milk from his cows. The _____ milking time is very early.

6. Three huge barns hold the animals. Painting the _____ walls is a hard job.

> ■ The **verb** is the main word in the predicate. If the verb tells an action that the subject is doing, it is called an **action verb**.
>   EXAMPLES: Children **play** in the park. The squirrel **ran** up the tree.

A. Underline the action verb in each sentence.

1. Rex jumped at Tiger.
2. Tiger leaped for the tree.
3. Rex snapped back at the end of his rope.
4. Tiger quickly spun around.
5. Tiger arched her back.
6. Rex pulled against his rope.
7. Tiger danced sideways.
8. Rex howled loudly.
9. Then Tiger licked a furry paw.
10. She yawned slowly.
11. Rex chewed at the old rope.
12. He snarled at the cat.
13. Tiger teased Rex even more.
14. Rex pulled against the rope again.
15. Suddenly, it snapped.
16. Tiger shot into the air.
17. Rex bounded across the yard.
18. Tiger scrambled up the tree just in time.

B. Complete each sentence by adding a predicate with an action verb to each subject.

1. The captain of the team _____

2. The coach _____

3. All of the team members _____

4. The fans _____

5. The scorekeeper _____

6. Everyone _____

Linking Verbs

■ A **linking verb** does not show action. Instead, it links the subject to a word that either describes the subject or gives the subject another name. If a verb can be replaced by one of the verbs of being (am, is, are, was, were), then it is a linking verb.

EXAMPLES: Football **is** exciting. (Exciting describes football.)
They **were** a tired group. (Group is another name for They.)
Yoko **grew** tired. (Grew can be replaced by is without changing the sentence.)

A. Complete each sentence with a different linking verb from the box.

are	feel	is	seem	sound
become	grow	look	smells	taste

1. Spring _____ a wonderful time of year.

2. The days _____ warm.

3. The air _____ fresh.

4. The flowers _____ pretty.

5. The evenings _____ lighter.

6. Spring vegetables _____ fresh.

7. The birds _____ cheerful.

8. We _____ more active.

B. Write L in front of each sentence that has a linking verb.

_____ 1. The day seemed dreary.

_____ 2. We decided to stay inside.

_____ 3. It was too cold and rainy outdoors.

_____ 4. Jenny started a roaring fire.

_____ 5. We were warm and cosy.

_____ 6. We felt comfortable.

> ■ A **helping verb** is sometimes used to help the main verb of a
> sentence. Helping verbs are often forms of the verb to be – am,
> is, are, was, were. The verbs has, have, and had are also used
> as helping verbs.   EXAMPLES: Jerry **has** gone to the store.
>   I am watching for the bus.

■ **Circle the helping verb and underline the main verb in each sentence.**

1. For a long time, we had wanted to give Sherry a surprise party.

2. We had planned the party in the park the day before her birthday.

3. She has gone to the park almost every day.

4. We were waiting for her there.

5. Sherry was raking her yard.

6. We were looking around the park for her.

7. We couldn't find her.

8. We were forced to make other plans.

9. So Sherry was given her surprise party on her birthday.

10. Juana is going to the zoo today.

11. She has gone there once before.

12. Jack had told her to see the monkeys.

13. She was going last week.

14. She had planned a picnic.

15. I am going to the zoo with her.

16. I have seen the zoo before.

17. We are taking the bus.

18. Jack is meeting us there.

19. He is riding his bike.

20. We are looking forward to our zoo visit.

Verb Tenses

> ■ The **tense** of a verb tells the time expressed by the verb. There are three tenses – present, past, and future.
> ■ **Present tense** tells about what is happening now.
>   EXAMPLE: I **am walking** my dog. I **walk** my dog.
> ■ **Past tense** tells about something that happened before.
>   EXAMPLE: I **walked** my dog yesterday.
> ■ **Future tense** tells about something that will happen.
>   EXAMPLE: I **will walk** my dog tonight.

A. Write present, past, or future to tell the tense of each underlined verb.

_____ 1. Jules Verne <u>wrote</u> about going to the moon.

_____ 2. Spaceships <u>were</u> still in the future.

_____ 3. Now we <u>can fly</u> to the moon.

_____ 4. A space shuttle <u>will lift</u> off tomorrow.

_____ 5. It <u>will carry</u> three astronauts.

_____ 6. The shuttle <u>helped</u> us explore space.

_____ 7. It <u>will help</u> us settle in space.

_____ 8. The shuttle <u>is taking</u> off now.

_____ 9. It <u>will return</u> in a week.

_____ 10. I <u>will watch</u> it land on TV.

_____ 11. It <u>will be</u> a sight to remember.

B. Complete each sentence by writing a verb in the tense shown in parentheses.

(past)   1. Joy _____ in the garden.

(present)   2. She _____ gardening.

(future)   3. The garden _____ many vegetables.

(present)   4. Joy _____ the garden to be nice.

(future)   5. She _____ flowers next week.

(past)   6. She _____ the garden last week.

- The past tense of a **regular verb** is usually formed by adding -ed.
  - EXAMPLE: jump – jumped
- If the word ends with a single consonant that has one vowel before it, double the final consonant and add -ed.
  - EXAMPLE: skip – skipped
- If the word ends with a silent e, drop the e and add -ed.
  - EXAMPLE: bake – baked
- If the root word ends in y, change the y to i and add -ed.
  - EXAMPLE: worry – worried

A. Write the past tense of each verb to complete each sentence.

1. Ms. Willis (look) _____ out the window.

2. She (gasp) _____ at what she saw.

3. A hot-air balloon (settle) _____ onto her lawn.

4. Two men (step) _____ from the balloon.

5. Ms. Willis (hurry) _____ across the yard.

6. The balloon's basket (crush) _____ her flower bed.

7. One man (scratch) _____ his head in wonder.

8. He said they were (head) _____ for the fairgrounds.

9. The wind had (change) _____ .

10. "We (drop) _____ in here instead," he said.

B. Rewrite each phrase in the past tense.

1. sail the boat

_____

2. steer a straight course

_____

3. carry the sail

_____

4. enjoy the fresh air and sunshine

_____

> ■ Do not add -ed to form the past tense of **irregular verbs**.
> Change the spelling in a different way.   EXAMPLES:
>
> | Present | Past | Present | Past | Present | Past |
> |---------|------|---------|------|---------|------|
> | begin | began | give | gave | say | said |
> | break | broke | go | went | see | saw |
> | choose | chose | grow | grew | sit | sat |
> | come | came | know | knew | take | took |
> | fall | fell | leave | left | throw | threw |
> | fly | flew | run | ran | write | wrote |

■ **Complete each sentence by writing the past tense of the verb in parentheses.**

1. Monday I (go) _____ to a singing tryout.

2. I got up and (leave) _____ the house early.

3. I (take) _____ the address but couldn't find the building.

4. Finally, I (know) _____ I needed to ask for directions.

5. I (grow) _____ worried that I would miss my turn.

6. Then I (see) _____ a sign on a building.

7. It (give) _____ a list of the companies in the building.

8. I (sit) _____ on a bench for a few minutes to calm down.

9. I (come) _____ to the right place after all.

10. Then I (fly) _____ upstairs to the office.

11. A man at the front desk frowned and (say) _____ I was late.

12. He (begin) _____ by handing me a form.

13. I (write) _____ my name, address, and phone number.

14. Then the pencil lead (break) _____ .

15. He took it from me and (throw) _____ it away.

16. I (choose) _____ another one from his desk.

17. On the way back to my chair, I slipped and (fall) _____ .

18. The man (run) _____ to help me.

Making Subjects and Verbs Agree

> ■ The **subject** and **verb** of a sentence must agree in number.
> ■ A **singular** subject must have a singular verb.
> ■ A **plural** subject must have a plural verb.
> ■ <u>You</u> and <u>I</u> must have a plural verb.
>   EXAMPLES: Mike **hits**. They **hit**. I **hit**. You **hit**.
> ■ The singular form of a verb usually ends in -<u>s</u> or -<u>es</u>. Add -<u>es</u> to verbs that end in -<u>s</u>, -<u>x</u>, -<u>z</u>, -<u>sh</u>, and -<u>ch</u>.
>   EXAMPLES: Juan **watches** the game. Amy **waxes** the car.

■ **Circle the verb that agrees with the subject of each sentence. Write singular or plural to show the number of the subject and verb.**

1. Chickens (**eat**, eats) grain. _____plural_____

2. A chicken (lives, live) on the ground. _____

3. They (flies, fly) very little. _____

4. A farmer (feeds, feed) the chickens every day. _____

5. Chickens (scratches, scratch) the ground for food. _____

6. Forest fires (causes, cause) damage every year. _____

7. A forest fire (destroys, destroy) large areas. _____

8. People (fights, fight) a fire with water and chemicals. _____

9. A firebreak (slows, slow) down a fire. _____

10. A river (acts, act) as a firebreak. _____

11. Airplanes (drops, drop) water on forest fires. _____

12. A firefighter always (watches, watch) for danger. _____

13. High winds (spreads, spread) forest fires. _____

14. One forest fire (kills, kill) many trees. _____

15. Many animals (loses, lose) their homes. _____

16. A forest (need, needs) many seasons to recover.

17. Responsible people (helps, help) prevent forest fires. _____

Making Subjects and Linking Verbs Agree

> ■ A **linking verb** is either singular or plural. The linking verb must match the subject of the sentence in number.
>   EXAMPLES: Singular – The movie **is** shown twice daily.
>   Plural – Both movies **are** shown twice daily.
> ■ A linking verb can be in the present tense or past tense.
>   EXAMPLES: Present tense – The movie **is** shown twice daily.
>   Past tense – Both movies **were** shown twice daily.
> ■ Use there is or there was with one person, place, or thing.
> ■ Use there are or there were with more than one.
>   EXAMPLES: There **is** a movie tonight. There **are** many movies showing at that theatre.

A. Write am, is, are, was, or were to complete each sentence.

1. My cat _____was_____ in the garden one day.

2. As I watched her, I _____ sure she wiggled her whiskers.

3. Her whiskers _____ shorter when she was a kitten.

4. A whisker _____ an organ of touch.

5. Whiskers _____ important to a cat.

6. My cat's whiskers _____ very long.

7. Her fur _____ very long, too.

8. I think my cat _____ beautiful!

B. Write There is, There are, There was, or There were to complete each sentence.

1. _____ many kinds of horses.

2. _____ no horses in North America at one time.

3. _____ a horse called the pinto that looks painted.

4. _____ many famous pintos.

5. _____ pinto horse clubs that you can join today.

6. _____ a national pinto horse club meeting every year.

7. _____ people working to save the pinto horse.

8. _____ a good reason for this – they are beautiful animals.

Unit 3, Grammar and Usage   © 1997 Gage Educational Publishing Company   **39**

Lesson 32
Subject Pronouns

- A **pronoun** is a word that takes the place of a noun.
- A **subject pronoun** is used as the subject of a sentence or as part of the subject of a sentence. The subject pronouns are I, you, he, she, it, we, and they.

  EXAMPLES: **We** went to class. Shelly and **I** did homework together. **He** is going to help us.

A. Underline the subject pronoun in each sentence.

1. She rode her bike almost every day.
2. It was a beautiful mountain bike.
3. They go as fast as the wind.
4. You can go anywhere on a bike like that.
5. We wanted to ride the bike.
6. I asked for a ride.
7. He got to ride first.
8. Then I got to ride.

B. Complete each sentence by writing a subject pronoun to replace the word or words in parentheses. Pretend you are Bill.

1. Mario and (Bill) _____I_____ left early for school.
2. (Mario and I) _____ had a test to study for.
3. (Mario) _____ had studied, but I hadn't.
4. (The test) _____ was on plants.
5. (Plants) _____ are important to study.
6. "Which part are (Bill) _____ studying?" Mario asked.
7. (Mrs. Hobart) _____ says this is an important test.
8. (Bill) _____ am going to study hard.

C. Write three sentences of your own using subject pronouns.

1. _____
2. _____
3. _____

 Unit 3, Grammar and Usage

■ An **object pronoun** is used after an action verb or after words such as <u>to</u>, <u>with</u>, <u>for</u>, and <u>by</u>. The object pronouns are <u>me</u>, <u>you</u>, <u>him</u>, <u>her</u>, <u>it</u>, <u>us</u>, and <u>them</u>.   EXAMPLES: Jim told him to start. Alex bought the present for her.

A. Underline the object pronoun in each sentence.

1. Marlena won it in record time.

2. The speed of the run surprised us.

3. Jeff beat me by a mile.

4. Maria caught us in the last lap.

5. Wendy will give them the prize.

6. The speech will be made by you.

7. Then a special prize will be given to him.

8. Wendy told me the prize is a blue ribbon.

B. Complete each sentence by writing an object pronoun to replace the word or words in parentheses.

1. The teacher told (I) _____ to read my report.

2. I told (Mr. Sheen) _____ that the report wasn't ready.

3. Mr. Sheen asked when (the report) _____ would be finished.

4. He had warned (our class) _____ that the reports were due.

5. Some of (the reports) _____ were done.

6. A few students offered to read (their reports) _____ .

7. The class listened to (Sonja) _____ .

8. Mr. Sheen said he wanted (the reports) _____ all finished by Friday.

C. Write four sentences of your own using object pronouns.

1. _____

2. _____

3. _____

4. _____

- Remember that a pronoun is a word that takes the place of a noun.
- A subject pronoun is used as the subject of a sentence.
- An object pronoun is used after an action verb, or after words such as <u>to</u>, <u>with</u>, <u>for</u>, and <u>by</u>.
  EXAMPLE: **Sam** gave **the gift** to **the boys**. **He** gave **it** to **them**.

- **Choose the correct pronoun to replace the underlined nouns in each sentence. Then rewrite each sentence, using the pronoun. You may use a pronoun more than once.**

| He | she | It | him | her | They | them | We | us |

1. <u>Helma and I</u> decided to attend the talk series at the library.

   _____

2. <u>The talks</u> would be every Wednesday evening for three weeks.

   _____

3. <u>The first one</u> was about the solar system.

   _____

4. We knew we would enjoy all of <u>the talks</u>.

   _____

5. Outer space has always been an interesting topic to <u>Helma and me</u>.

   _____

6. <u>The professor</u> was an excellent speaker.

   _____

7. The audience listened closely to <u>the speaker</u>.

   _____

8. Helma said the talk was one of the best <u>Helma</u> had ever heard.

   _____

9. The new facts we learned surprised <u>Helma</u>.

   _____

10. In fact, they surprised <u>Helma and me</u> both.

   _____

Lesson 35

Possessive Pronouns

> ■ A **possessive pronoun** is used to show who or what owns something. <u>My</u>, <u>our</u>, <u>your</u>, <u>his</u>, <u>her</u>, <u>its</u>, and <u>their</u> are possessive pronouns.
>   EXAMPLES: Is this **your** coat? **His** cold is getting better.

■ **Complete each sentence by writing the correct possessive pronoun.**

1. _____ family and I were going camping.

2. Suddenly _____ car stalled in a dark forest.

3. _____ engine just would not run.

4. _____ family was stuck.

5. Richard almost lost _____ temper.

6. He didn't expect this from _____ car.

7 Julie spoke, and _____ voice made everyone quiet.

8. We held _____ tongues.

9. "_____ hands are trembling," Richard said to Julie.

10. "So are _____ hands," Julie answered.

11. "Look at the bears with _____ paws up in the air," said Julie.

12. Richard tried to start _____ car.

13. Julie held _____ breath while the bears looked at us.

14. The mother bear turned _____ cubs toward the woods.

15. _____ growls could be heard through the car windows.

16. We hid _____ heads below the windows.

17. One cub turned _____ head toward us.

18. I tried to get _____ camera out, but I couldn't.

19. _____ strap was caught on something.

20. "You can tell _____ friends about your adventure when we get back," said Richard.

Adjectives

> ■ An **adjective** is a word that describes a noun. Adjectives tell
> **which one**, **what kind**, or **how many**.
> EXAMPLES: **happy** person, **brown** dog, **four** cars

A. Circle the two adjectives in each sentence.

1. The big cat chased the tiny mouse.
2. His sharp teeth flashed in the bright light.
3. The scared mouse ran through the small hole.
4. The speeding cat slipped on the wet floor.
5. The tired mouse hid in a dark corner.
6. The damp cat left in a big hurry.
7. The little mouse had a wide smile.

B. Add an adjective to each sentence in these paragraphs.

beautiful	green	Many	sparkling
fierce	dark	Gentle	Wild

_____ people go to the _____

national parks. They see _____ streams and

_____ forests. _____ animals roam

freely on _____ meadows. _____

deer and _____ bears both live in the forests.

bare	red	shaky	soft	thick
best	wooden	six	strong	young

The _____ man climbed the _____ ladder. A

_____ wind blew the _____ branches. His

_____ friend steadied the _____ ladder. He picked

_____ _____ apples. The _____ leaves

tickled his _____ arm.

Adjectives That Compare

> - Sometimes adjectives are used to compare one thing to another.
> - Most adjectives that compare two things end in -er.
>   EXAMPLE: The red chair is **bigger** than the blue chair.
> - Most adjectives that compare more than two things end in -est.
>   EXAMPLE: That chair is the **biggest** chair in the store.

A. Circle the correct adjective in each sentence.

1. Jean's puppy is the (smaller, smallest) of all the puppies.

2. He is (smaller, smallest) than his brother.

3. Toby was the (cuter, cutest) name Jean could think of.

4. Toby looked (funnier, funniest) than his sister.

5. He had the (whiter, whitest) fur of all the puppies.

6. Toby had the (longer, longest) ears Jean had ever seen.

7. Jean soon learned that Toby was the (naughtier, naughtiest) puppy she had ever known.

8. He played (harder, hardest) than his brother.

9. He stayed awake (later, latest) than his sister.

10. He kept Jean (busier, busiest) than the mother dog.

11. He was the (happier, happiest) puppy in the litter.

12. But he'll never be the (bigger, biggest) dog.

B. Add -er or -est to the end of each adjective to complete the sentences.

1. Tim's hair is light _____ than Jamie's.

2. Who has the dark _____ hair in class?

3. Ida has straight _____ hair than Tina.

4. Tina has the wild _____ hairdo of all.

5. Is her hair long _____ than Jamie's?

6. February is the short _____ month of the year.

7. January is long _____ than June.

8. July is warm _____ than February.

9. March is cold _____ than July.

10. Which do you think is the cold _____ month of all?

© 1997 Gage Educational Publishing Company

■ An **adverb** is a word that describes a verb. Adverbs tell **how**, **when**, or **where**. Many adverbs end in -ly.
EXAMPLES: He ran **quickly**. She was sad **today**.
Water dripped **here yesterday**.

A. Circle the two adverbs in each sentence.

1. It was widely known that he would cheerfully fix anything.

2. Yesterday he was calmly asked to repair a faucet.

3. He quickly and loudly refused.

4. Later, he quietly apologized for his response.

B. Circle the adverb in each sentence. Then write how, when, or where to show what the adverb tells about the word it describes.

_____ 1. Yuri walked quietly.

_____ 2. He sang softly as he walked.

_____ 3. Later, he ate lunch.

_____ 4. He sat there to eat.

C. Use adverbs from the list below to complete the sentences.

anxiously	quickly	Suddenly
brightly	loudly	there
desperately	purposefully	very

1. _____ , Sam ran to the door.

2. He ran _____ into the street.

3. The sun shone _____ .

4. He looked _____ at his watch.

5. He began to walk _____ .

6. He knew he was _____ late for the party.

7. He tried _____ to make it to the party on time.

8. Finally he got _____ .

9. He knocked _____ , then joined the party.

Adverbs That Compare

> - **Adverbs**, like adjectives, can be used to compare two or more things.
> - Most adverbs that compare two things end in -er.
>   EXAMPLE: I arrived **sooner** than you did.
> - Most adverbs that compare more than two things end in -est.
>   EXAMPLE: Ted runs the **fastest** of all the team members.
> - Sometimes more is used with a longer adverb when comparing two things. Sometimes most is used with a longer adverb when comparing more than two things.
>   EXAMPLES: I drove **more carefully** than John. Tim drove **most carefully** of all.

A. Circle the correct adverb in each sentence.

1. Jean worked (faster, fastest) than Debbie.

2. Debbie finished (later, latest) than Jean.

3. Of all the workers, Donna worked the (later, latest).

4. She wanted to be done (sooner, soonest) than Jean.

5. Debbie worked (more carefully, most carefully) of all.

6. No one tried (harder, hardest) than Debbie.

B. Complete each sentence by writing the correct form of each adverb in parentheses.

1. The swans arrived (late) _____ than the ducks.

2. Of all the birds, they flew the (quietly) _____ .

3. The duck quacked (loudly) _____ than the swan.

4. The swan swam (peacefully) _____ than the duck.

5. The beautiful black swan swam the (near) _____ to me of all the birds.

6. He swam (slowly) _____ than the white swan.

7. I will be back here (soon) _____ than you.

8. The picture of the swans will be taken (carefully)

_____ than my other picture.

- Good is an adjective that describes nouns. <u>Well</u> is an adverb that tells how something is done.
  EXAMPLE: That is a **good** TV that works **well**.

A. Use <u>good</u> or <u>well</u> to complete each sentence.

1. George sings _____ , and Jill is a _____ dancer. ·

2. They work _____ together.

3. Both George and Jill had _____ teachers.

4. They learned _____ from their teachers.

5. They perform their act _____ .

6. Their piano music is very _____ , too.

7. They both play the piano very _____ .

8. Such _____ performers are hard to find.

9. Everyone who sees them perform has a _____ time.

10. I'm going to practise so that I can sing as _____ as George.

11. Don't you think that's a _____ idea?

- Do not use a <u>no</u> word with another <u>no</u> word or after a contraction that ends with -n't. Some <u>no</u> words are <u>no</u>, <u>none</u>, <u>nobody</u>, <u>nothing</u>, <u>nowhere</u>, <u>never</u>, and <u>not</u>.
  EXAMPLES: Incorrect – **Nobody never** writes me letters.
  Correct – **Nobody ever** writes me letters.

B. Circle the correct word to complete each sentence.

1. The boy doesn't have (no, any) paper.

2. I haven't (no, any) extra paper for him to borrow.

3. The teacher has (nothing, anything) to give him, either.

4. Doesn't he (ever, never) bring extra paper?

5. Are you sure you don't have (no, any) paper?

6. Hasn't someone got (nothing, something) to give him?

7. Why doesn't (anybody, nobody) ever plan ahead?

Using Other Words Correctly

> - <u>Those</u> is an adjective used to describe a noun. <u>Them</u> is an object pronoun and is used after a verb or a word such as <u>at</u>, <u>with</u>, <u>to</u>, and <u>for</u>.
>   EXAMPLES: I like **those** shoes. I'd like to buy **them**.

A. Write <u>them</u> or <u>those</u> to complete each sentence.

1. Did you see _____ boys?

2. I have not seen _____ this afternoon.

3. If I do see _____ , I'll give _____ a speech.

4. Have you seen _____ models all over their room?

5. I told _____ to put _____ models away yesterday.

6. I'd better find _____ soon.

7. Otherwise, I might make _____ models disappear!

8. I am not happy with _____ boys at all!

> - Doesn't is singular. Use <u>doesn't</u> with one person, place, or thing.
> - Don't is plural. Use <u>don't</u> with more than one and with the words <u>you</u> and I.
>   EXAMPLES: Ed **doesn't** have a ride home. We **don't** have room in the car.

B. Write <u>doesn't</u> or <u>don't</u> to complete each sentence.

1. Juan and Charles _____ want to miss the rehearsal.

2. Charles _____ like to be late.

3. Kirin thinks it _____ matter if they're late.

4. Jamie _____ seem to care if he goes to rehearsal.

5. Juan and Charles _____ understand why he _____ want to go.

6. The director _____ want anyone to miss a rehearsal.

7. He says they can't perform well if they _____ rehearse.

8. I _____ doubt that for a minute.

A. Circle the common nouns in each sentence. Underline the proper nouns. Draw a box around the possessive nouns.

1. Mark took his old car.
2. He drove to the town of Chester.
3. Jan lives on a farm nearby.
4. He wanted to ride her horse, Bullet.
5. Bullet is Jan's favourite pet.
6. She has a horse, two dogs, and a rabbit.
7. The rabbit, All Ears, lives in the horse's barn.
8. The dogs' home is under the front porch.

B. Write A, L, or H to tell if the underlined verb is an action, linking, or helping verb.

_____ 1. Tony is packing tonight.

_____ 2. He leaves tomorrow

_____ 3. Tony has always liked camping.

_____ 4. He seems happiest outdoors.

_____ 5. Tony was born in the city.

_____ 6. He grew used to walking everywhere.

_____ 7. Now he hikes outdoors for hours.

_____ 8. He carries with him everything he needs.

C. Complete each sentence by writing the underlined verb in the tense shown in parentheses.

(past) 1. Karina receive _____ her diploma.

(future) 2. Now she decide _____ what to do next.

(present) 3. _____ she choose to get a job?

(past) 4. She go _____ into landscaping.

(present) 5. Karina like _____ to plant things and watch them grow.

(past) 6. She grow _____ a wonderful garden for the city park.

 Unit 3, Grammar and Usage

D. Circle the verb that agrees with the subject of each sentence.

1. Recipes (is, are) directions for cooking.
2. (There is, There are) recipes for almost every type of food.
3. Some people (follow, follows) recipes each time they cook.
4. My grandmother rarely (use, used) one.
5. I always thought she (is, was) the best cook I ever knew.
6. (There was, There were) hundreds of recipes in her cookbook.
7. Her friends (was, were) always asking for her recipe for some dish.
8. She (give, gave) them her recipes, but not her cooking secrets.
9. Grandmother always (say, said) that only taste counted.
10. Recipes (is, are) fine to start with, but she always (add, added) something special.

E. Underline the pronouns in the sentences.

1. She gave him a book.
2. She bought it on sale.
3. Her favourite book is *The Secret World of Og*.
4. He is reading it now and likes it.
5. She hoped he would be pleased.
6. They like to share their books.
7. She is finishing a mystery.
8. Then he will read it.
9. Science fiction books are his choice.
10. But she thinks he will like Encyclopedia Brown, too.

F. Circle the adjective or adverb in each sentence. Then write <u>adjective</u> or <u>adverb</u> on the lines.

_____ 1. Megan Follows is a Canadian actress.

_____ 2. Her dazzling smile makes others smile, too.

_____ 3. Some say she is a wonderful actress.

_____ 4. She is a bigger star than others her age.

_____ 5. Megan quickly rose to fame.

_____ 6. Later she dropped out of movies for a while.

_____ 7. She has acted at the famous Stratford Festival.

_____ 8. So far she has handled fame better than I would.

A. Read the paragraph. Then follow the directions.

As he stands outside the old house, Marty wonders if this is a good idea. He wants to go in, but the history of the house stops him. All of the people in Charlesville know of Mr. Bremmer and this place. Marty starts to walk toward the door. He still wonders if he should.

1. List the nouns from the paragraph in the correct column.

Common	Proper
_____	_____
_____	_____
_____	_____
_____	
_____	
_____	

2. Rewrite the paragraph in the past tense.

_____

_____

_____

_____

_____

B. Circle the correct verb. Rewrite the sentences.

1. Some jobs (is, are) not worth the money.

_____

2. We (agree, agrees) with that.

_____

3. Whoever (watch, watches) this place must be brave.

_____

4. Marty (is, are) not sure that he (is, are) brave enough.

_____

52   **Unit 3, Grammar and Usage**

C. Rewrite the paragraph. Replace the underlined nouns with pronouns.

Marty got up Marty's nerve and walked to the house. The front of the house was dark. There were faces carved in the stone. The faces looked mean. "The faces are strange," Marty thought. The faces scared Marty. "Oh well, here I go," Marty said to himself.

_____

_____

_____

_____

D. Choose one adjective and one adverb to complete each sentence.

Adjectives		**Adverbs**	
noisy	scariest	barely	slowly
brighter	shaky	ever	strangely
rusty		quieter	

1. The _____ doorknob turned _____ .

2. This was the _____ job he had _____ taken.

3. Except for the _____ doorknob, it was _____ than a library.

4. His _____ hand _____ touched the cobweb when he saw something awful.

5. Eyes _____ than fire were staring _____ from the corner.

E. Circle the correct words to complete the paragraph.

"This (don't, doesn't) look good," Marty mumbled to himself. (Them, Those) eyes belong to something. I (don't, doesn't) remember (never, ever) seeing (nothing, anything) like those eyes before. If I get out of here, I'll learn my lesson (good, well). You won't (ever, never) find me in a place like this again."

> ■ **Capitalize** the names of people and pets.
>   EXAMPLES: Dennis Lee has written many poems. Did
>   he have a son named Nicholas?
> ■ Capitalize family names.
>   EXAMPLES: Uncle Bob married Aunt Margie.
>   Mom and Dad got married in India.

■ **Rewrite these sentences using capital letters where needed.**

1. uncle george got up early today.

_____

2. He and aunt beth had a special job to do.

_____

3. uncle george and aunt beth were going to the animal shelter.

_____

4. They wanted to find a puppy for susan and michael.

_____

5. uncle george and aunt beth thought a small dog would be nice.

_____

6. But susan and michael wanted a big dog.

_____

7. uncle george saw a cute kitten named mittens.

_____

8. In the very last cage, they saw sasha.

_____

9. uncle george and aunt beth loved her at once.

_____

10. When sasha ran circles around michael, he loved her, too.

_____

Lesson 43

Capitalizing Names of Places and Things

> - Capitalize each word in a place name.
>   EXAMPLES: Moose Jaw, Germany, Manitoba,
>   Westwood School, Wm. Main Library, Red River
> - Capitalize days of the week, months of the year, holidays, and names of monuments.
>   EXAMPLES: Tuesday, February, Valentine's Day,
>   the Cenotaph

A. Rewrite these sentences using capital letters where needed.

1. Our family will spend labour day in ottawa.

   _____

2. We hope to see the parliament buildings and the peace tower.

   _____

3. We also want to see the museum of civilization.

   _____

4. The ottawa river forms a border between ottawa and hull.

   _____

5. The peacekeeper's monument is amazing.

   _____

6. The national gallery gets many visitors.

   _____

7. There are many amazing sights in ottawa.

   _____

B. Answer these questions. Use capital letters where needed.

1. When were you born?

   _____

2. What is your address? Include the city and province.

   _____

3. What is your favourite holiday?

   _____

> - Capitalize the first, last, and all important words in a book title. Words such as <u>a</u>, <u>an</u>, <u>and</u>, <u>but</u>, <u>by</u>, <u>for</u>, <u>in</u>, <u>of</u>, <u>on</u>, <u>from</u>, <u>the</u>, and <u>to</u> are not considered important words. They are not capitalized unless one of them is the first word in the title. Underline all titles of books.
>   EXAMPLE: <u>A Present from Rosita</u>
> - Capitalize titles of respect.
>   EXAMPLES: Major Thomas, Doctor Freeman

A. Rewrite these names and titles correctly. Underline the book titles.

1. doctor phillip h. chan _____

2. judge rosa allen _____

3. The book: a wrinkle in time _____

4. captain william faircroft _____

5. prime minister jean chrétien _____

6. doctor laurie c. bell _____

7. The book: attack of the monster plants _____

8. major carol gates _____

9. The book: owls in the family _____

10. The book: my side of the mountain _____

B. Circle each letter that should be capitalized. Write the capital letter above it. Underline the book titles.

1. In 1845, sir john franklin and his crew disappeared while exploring arctic waters.

2. One of the many who tried to find them was captain richard collinson.

3. Finally doctor john rae found they had all perished near King William Island.

4. A century later, professor owen beattie discovered why they died.

5. You can read about it in his book, buried in ice.

Lesson 45

Capitalizing Abbreviations

- Capitalize **abbreviations** of days and months.
    EXAMPLES: Sun., Mon., Tues., Wed., Thurs., Fri., Sat.
    November – Nov., August – Aug.
- Capitalize abbreviations for titles of respect.
    EXAMPLES: Mr., Mrs., Dr.
- Capitalize an **initial**, the first letter of a name.
    EXAMPLE: T. J. Pavlicek

A. Write the correct abbreviation for the days and months of the year.

1. Tuesday _____

2. Wednesday _____

3. Thursday _____

4. Friday _____

5. Saturday _____

6. Sunday _____

7. January _____

8. November _____

9. September _____

10. August _____

11. October _____

12. December _____

B. Rewrite these sentences using capital letters where needed.

1. The circus is coming on aug. 12.

_____

2. It will be held in wm. Wallace Arena.

_____

3. The amazing acrobat, j.c. Leblanc, will be there.

_____

4. Our teacher, ms. Foster, is taking the whole class.

_____

5. Many people will be at the arena on thurs.

_____

6. Even mr wong, the principal, will attend.

_____

7. On sun., aug. 15, the circus will travel to victoria, b.c.

_____

- Capitalize the street name, city, postal code, and date in a letter. Also capitalize all letters in abbreviations for provinces. Together these words make up the **heading**.

    EXAMPLE: 1100 N. Main St.
    Lindsay, ON K9P 6G4
    May 24, 1997

- Capitalize the **greeting**.

    EXAMPLE: Dear Mr. Jones,

- Capitalize the first word of the **closing**.

    EXAMPLES: Sincerely yours, Your friend,

- **Underline the letters that should be capitalized in the letters.**

7216 melvin street

brandon, mb r7b 2m3

October 23, 1997

dear fred,

   I am doing a report on farm life. Do you have any information you can send me? My report must be turned in three weeks from today. I can really use any help you can give me. Pictures and facts would be helpful. The names of some books I could find at the library would also help a lot.

       your friend,

       jesse

---

820 w. jubilee dr.

regina, sk s4x 1g3

October 29, 1997

dear jesse,

   I'll be glad to help with your report. Better yet, why don't you come and visit? Call and let me know if you are coming. The library here has lots of information. I know we could find everything you need for your project.

       your friend,

       fred

- Begin all sentences with a capital letter.
  EXAMPLE: Mary rode a bike.
- End a statement or a command with a **period. (.)**
  EXAMPLE: Jake rode a bike.
- End a question with a **question mark. (?)**
  EXAMPLE: Did Jake ride a bike?
- End an exclamation with an **exclamation point. (!)**
  EXAMPLE: Ouch, I fell!

A. Begin and end each sentence correctly. Put the correct punctuation mark at the end of each sentence, and circle any letters that should be capitalized.

1. i am going to ride my bike to the store
2. where is my bike
3. it is always in the garage
4. could it be on the back porch
5. i'll ask Joanne if she has seen it
6. she said it was in the garage this morning
7. oh, no, someone has stolen my bike
8. what should I do now
9. who could have taken it

B. Rewrite each sentence correctly.

1. i'll call the police about my bike

_____

2. hurry, hurry, answer the phone

_____

3. hello, is this the police station

_____

4. yes, what can we do for you

_____

5. you must help me catch a bike thief

_____

6. how do you know your bike wasn't borrowed

_____

> - Use a **comma (,)** to take the place of the word <u>and</u> when three or more things are listed together in a sentence.
>   EXAMPLE: Maya, Pete, and George went to the beach.
> - Use a comma to separate the parts of a compound sentence.
>   EXAMPLE: Mary drove her car, but Peter walked.
> - Use a comma to set off words such as <u>yes</u>, <u>no</u>, and <u>well</u> at the beginning of a sentence.
>   EXAMPLE: Yes, I want to ride my bike.

- **Rewrite these sentences using commas correctly. Leave out the word <u>and</u> when possible.**

1. I called Ajay and Janet and Karen last Saturday.

   _____

2. Yes they wanted to have a picnic.

   _____

3. Ajay packed a lunch and Karen brought a backpack.

   _____

4. Well we were finally ready to go.

   _____

5. Yes we found a perfect place by the beach.

   _____

6. We played volleyball and swam and hiked.

   _____

7. It was a great picnic and there were no ants around.

   _____

8. We collected shells and driftwood and pebbles.

   _____

9. Ajay cleaned up the garbage and Karen packed the leftovers.

   _____

10. We sang and laughed and read.

    _____

- Use a comma to set off the name of a person spoken to.
  EXAMPLE: Pam, you said we could go.
- Use commas to set off a phrase that helps explain the subject of a sentence.
  EXAMPLE: Mr. Gonzales, Rudy's father, is a lawyer.

A. Add commas where needed in each sentence.

1. Our neighbour Buddy Rush is missing.
2. Mr. Rush his father says he doesn't know where Buddy is.
3. Danny did Buddy talk about going somewhere?
4. This seems very strange to me Tim.
5. Ms. Carter our teacher thinks so, too.
6. Buddy where are you?
7. There he is Mr. Rush!
8. Buddy the silly goose fell asleep in his treehouse!

B. Put an X in front of the sentence that tells about each numbered sentence.

1. Craig, your brother is here.

   _____ Craig is your brother.

   _____ Someone is talking to Craig.

2. Lydia, my friend will go, too.

   _____ Lydia is my friend.

   _____ Someone is talking to Lydia.

3. Our neighbour, Mrs. Hicks, is sick.

   _____ Mrs. Hicks is our neighbour.

   _____ Someone is talking to your neighbour.

4. Carrie, your sister is home.

   _____ Carrie is your sister.

   _____ Someone is talking to Carrie.

5. Anna, my dog, is loose.

   _____ Anna is my dog.

   _____ Someone is talking to Anna.

> ■ Use a comma between the city and province in the heading.
> Use a comma between the day and year.
>   EXAMPLE: 872 Park Street
>   Vancouver, BC V6B 7R9
>   September 17, 1997
> ■ Use a comma following the name in the greeting.
>   EXAMPLES: Dear Nancy, Dear Mr. Muller,
> ■ Use a comma following the last word of the closing.
>   EXAMPLE: Sincerely yours,

A. Add commas where needed in the letters.

5th Ave. S.

Lethbridge AB T1K 3M8

November 12 1997

Dear Mark

    Thank you for coming to my party. It was fun having you there. I also want to thank you for the great sweatshirt. It fits fine, and I really like it.

Your friend

Theresa

---

765 Queen's Rd.

Lethbridge AB T1F 4G6

November 16 1997

Dear Theresa

    Don't forget about the trip to the museum on Saturday. See you there.

Sincerely

Mark

B. Add commas where they are needed in the headings.

1. 321 Gatineau Blvd.
Timmins ON P4R 1E2
November 17 1997

2. 101 Wellington St.
Sherbrooke PQ J1E 7R9
July 10 1997

C. Add commas where they are needed in the greetings and closings.

1. Dear Josée

2. Sincerely yours

3. Your friend

4. Dear Grandmother

5. Your grandson

6. Hi, Sacha

- A **quote** tells the exact words someone says. Put **quotation marks (" ")** before and after the words. Use a comma, a period, a question mark, or an exclamation point between the quoted words and the rest of the sentence. Begin the first word of a direct quote with a capital letter.
    EXAMPLES: "Why don't you eat your cereal?" asked Jack.
    Jenny said, "I'm not hungry."

- **Look at the pictures. See who is talking and what is being said. Tell what each speaker said. Include the word <u>said</u> or <u>asked</u> and the name of the speaker. Add quotation marks and commas where needed.**

Ms. Riley

> Do you want to talk about the interesting places we each visited this summer?

> My sister and I visited my aunt in Banff, Alberta.

James

Jenny

> We flew to Québec to see our Grandmother.

> We went camping in Algonquin Park.

Dorothy

1. What did Ms. Riley say?

"Do you want to talk about the interesting places we each

visited this summer?"

2. What did James say?

_____

3. What did Jenny say?

_____

4. What did Dorothy say?

_____

- Sometimes the speaker of a quote is named in the middle of the words being spoken. When this happens, quotation marks should be placed before and after both groups of words. Commas are placed inside the quotation marks at the end of the first group of words and again after the speaker's name.
  EXAMPLE: "I'd like to go," said Mary, "but I can't."

- **Place quotation marks around the quotes. Add question marks and commas where needed.**

1. Well said Costa Dot is just getting over a strange accident.

2. What happened asked Susan.

3. A thought struck her said Costa.

4. Jake asked Why did you throw the alarm clock out the window

5. Because said Rita I wanted to see time fly.

6. What did one wall say to another asked Bonnie.

7. I'll meet you at the corner answered David.

8. What gets wetter Carlos asked the more you dry

9. A towel does said Angie.

10. Mother said Are your feet dirty

11. Yes replied Bobby but don't worry because I have my shoes on.

12. Maria asked How can you tell when an ice cube is nervous

13. It breaks out said Bill in a cold sweat.

14. Anna asked What is black-and-white and red all over

15. It's a blushing zebra said Jake.

16. What did the rug say to the floor asked Costa.

17. Don't move replied Bonnie because I've got you covered.

18. Rita asked Why do sponges do a good job

19. They become absorbed in their work said Carlos.

20. Angie asked Why is a pencil like a riddle

21. Because said Maria it's no good without a point.

> - Use an **apostrophe (')** in a contraction to show where a letter or letters are taken out.
> - <u>Won't</u> is an exception. will not = won't
> - Contractions can be made by joining a verb and <u>not</u>.
>   EXAMPLES: can not = can't, did not = didn't
> - Contractions can also be made by joining a noun or pronoun and a verb.
>   EXAMPLES: **It's** (it + is) a beautiful day.
>   **Susan's** (Susan + is) going to the park.
>   **She'll** (she + will) have a lot of fun.

A. Circle the correct meaning for the contraction in each sentence.

1. Donna said she'll go to the store today.   (she will, she had)

2. We're supposed to clean the house.   (We will, We are)

3. Beth and James say they'll clean the living room, too.

   (they will, they would)

4. I'll clean the kitchen.   (I would, I will)

5. She's going to be home soon.   (She is, She will)

6. We'd better get moving!   (We will, We had)

B. Write the contraction for the underlined words.

1. <u>It is</u> funny that <u>we are</u> lost.

   _____   _____

2. <u>You are</u> sure <u>we have</u> followed the directions correctly?

   _____   _____

3. <u>I am</u> sure <u>they will</u> start looking for us soon.

   _____   _____

4. We <u>did not</u> bring a map, but we <u>should have</u>.

   _____   _____

5. <u>I will</u> bet that <u>we will</u> be here all night.

   _____   _____

6. <u>We are</u> in trouble now because <u>I am</u> tired.

   _____   _____

Using Apostrophes to Show Possession

> ■ Remember that apostrophes are not only used in contractions.
> They are also used to show ownership, or possession.
> EXAMPLES: Contraction – My **sister's** coming here.
> Possessive – My **sister's** friend is coming here.
> Both my **sisters'** friends are coming.

A. Rewrite each word in parentheses to show ownership. Use -'s or -s'.

1. Our family went on a trip in my (brother) _____ car.

2. The (car) _____ windows would not roll down.

3. (Dad) _____ clothes were soaked with sweat.

4. Both my (sisters) _____ clothes were wrinkled.

5. Finally my (family) _____ terrible trip was over.

6. We arrived at our (friends) _____ house for our visit.

B. Rewrite each sentence. Replace each underlined phrase with a phrase that includes a possessive with an apostrophe.

1. We all liked the story Mei told the best.

   _____

2. The setting of the story was an old castle.

   _____

3. There was a prison in the basement of the castle.

   _____

4. The attention of the students was on Mei as she read.

   _____

5. A cruel man lived in the tower of the castle.

   _____

6. The children of the cruel man weren't allowed to play.

   _____

A. Circle the letters that need to be capitalized.

1. marjorie took her horse, blaze, out for a ride.

2. she rode through grandville to the miller house.

3. dr. miller's mother, mrs. miller, was the town's oldest living resident.

4. Mrs. miller has lived in grand county since 1915.

5. On oct. 10, she turned 100 years old.

6. She got a telegram from queen elizabeth.

7. marjorie and her friends loved to hear mrs. miller talk about her experiences.

B. Put a period, a question mark, or an exclamation point on the blank following each sentence. Add commas where needed.

5780 Smith Rd. W.

London ON N5Z 3B9

December 10 1997

Dear Pam

    It's been a long time since my last letter __ How are you __ Everything is fine here but I really miss having you as a neighbour __ Amy our new neighbour is nice __ She goes to our school and she is in my class __ No she will never replace you as my best friend __ Oh I almost forgot __ Mrs. Tandy said "Tell Pam hello for me __ " We all miss you a lot __ Do you still think you can visit this summer __

Your friend

Delia

C. Add quotation marks, commas, and other punctuation marks where needed.

1. Henry stand by the door for a minute said Raffi.

2. What for asked Henry.

3. I want you to hold the door answered Raffi while I bring in this table.

4. Henry asked Are you going to carry that by yourself?

5. It's not very heavy said Raffi.

6. What are you going to do with it asked Henry.

7. We need it for the kitchen said Raffi.

D. Rewrite each sentence correctly.

1. well it's time to get to work said lisa

   _____

2. lisa walked out of the room and jeremy followed her

   _____

3. lisa pointed to the trash can

   _____

4. what a mess jeremy cried

   _____

5. your dog did this said lisa

   _____

6. oh so now peanut's all mine said jeremy

   _____

7. yes when he's bad he's yours said lisa

   _____

8. they laughed and cleaned up the trash together

   _____

E. Rewrite each sentence. Use apostrophes where needed.

1. Wont the twins mother let them ride the Thunder Demon?

   _____

2. Ill bet its scary!

   _____

3. Roller coasters names dont usually sound comforting.

   _____

4. This ones seats arent very wide.

   _____

5. Perhaps Pauls sisters shouldnt go until theyre older.

   _____

6. Hes going with his best friends, James and Gino.

   _____

A. Circle letters that should be capitalized. Add needed commas, periods, exclamation points, quotation marks, and apostrophes.

miriam stone CKLBs top reporter woke up early. she said I have plenty of time to get ready. she thought of the letter she received yesterday:

920 lake st s.
kamloops bc v2b 7k6
april 1 1997

dear miriam

if you want a really exciting story, meet me at the j m banister library at ten o'clock tomorrow morning. I m sure your stations newsroom will want this story.

yours truly
A Fan

she asked herself what it could be. miriam dressed ate breakfast got her notebook and headed for the library. it was not far and soon she was there.

suddenly a short woman in a dark dress walked up and said I wrote the letter. she said you must hear my story.

my name is jessica she said. Ive been tricked by a gang of crooks. i need your help.

miriam said tell me your story and I'll see what I can do

jessica told miriam of a man named officer j c cook who said he worked for the rcmp. he told her he needed a key to all the safety boxes in the bank where she worked. yes she said it was strange but he said it was for national security. now all of the boxes had been robbed and she was sure it was officer cooks work.

miriam was excited about the story. now said miriam tell me everything you can remember about officer j c cook.

wow what a story miriam said excitedly

B. Rewrite the letter. Add capital letters, periods, question marks, exclamation points, commas, quotation marks, and apostrophes where needed.

420 station st
rosebud ab t0j 4a9
april 3 1997

dear mr thompson

i appreciate the time you spent with me tuesday __ i learned a great deal about thompsons freight lines and i am sure that i would do a good job for your company __ i have two years of experience in shipping goods around the world __

it was a pleasure to meet you and speak with you __ what a surprise to learn that you know my uncle joe so well __ he speaks very highly of you and your company __ thank you again for seeing me __ ill call you in a few days __

yours truly
wayne s carver

_____

_____

_____

_____

_____

_____

_____

_____

_____

_____

_____

_____

_____

- Remember that a **sentence** is a group of words that tells a complete thought.
- A sentence must have at least two parts – a subject and a predicate.

      S   P
EXAMPLE: <u>Sophie Pappas</u> <u>was bored</u>.

- **Read each group of words. Then answer the questions.**

1. Sophie needed a hobby.

    a. Is there a subject? _____   If so, what is it?_____

    b. Is there a predicate? _____   If so, what is it?_____

    c. Is there a complete thought? _____   Is this a sentence? _____

2. Sophie finally.

    a. Is there a subject? _____   If so, what is it?_____

    b. Is there a predicate? _____   If so, what is it?_____

    c. Is there a complete thought? _____   Is this a sentence? _____

3. Will do a family history.

    a. Is there a subject? _____   If so, what is it?_____

    b. Is there a predicate? _____   If so, what is it?_____

    c. Is there a complete thought? _____   Is this a sentence? _____

4. Sophie began planning.

    a. Is there a subject? _____   If so, what is it?_____

    b. Is there a predicate? _____   If so, what is it?_____

    c. Is there a complete thought? _____   Is this a sentence? _____

5. Asked questions.

    a. Is there a subject? _____   If so, what is it?_____

    b. Is there a predicate? _____   If so, what is it?_____

    c. Is there a complete thought? _____   Is this a sentence? _____

Lesson
56

Writing Topic Sentences

- A **paragraph** is a group of sentences about one main idea. There are usually several sentences in a paragraph. But sometimes a paragraph is only one sentence long. The first line of a paragraph is indented.
- A **topic sentence** is a sentence that tells the main idea of a paragraph. The topic sentence is usually the first sentence in a paragraph.

A. Read the paragraph. Underline the topic sentence.

Sophie decided that she needed a hobby. She thought about different things to pick for a hobby. She thought about collecting coins or stamps. Sophie finally chose to do a family history as her hobby.

B. Rewrite the sentences below in paragraph form. Put the topic sentence first and underline it. Remember to indent the first sentence.

1. To get the information she needed, Sophie would have to ask many questions.
2. She thought about the kinds of questions she would ask.
3. She wanted to make sure that she didn't forget any questions.
4. So Sophie wrote down a list of questions that she would ask each person.
5. Next she made copies of the list.
6. She put one person's name at the top of each copy.
7. Then she was ready to talk to people.

_____

_____

_____

_____

_____

_____

_____

_____

 Unit 5, Composition

> ■ Sentences with **supporting details** give more information about the main idea of a paragraph. Each sentence should contain details that support the topic sentence.

■ **Three sentences do not support the topic sentence. Draw a line through them. Then write the topic sentence and the five supporting sentences in paragraph form. Remember to indent the first sentence.**

Topic Sentence: Sophie was ready to begin her history.

1. First, she put her questions into a notebook.

2. She made sure she had pens and extra paper.

3. Then Sophie called Grandpa Casey and asked when she could come and talk to him.

4. She told Grandpa Casey about her new dog.

5. Grandpa Casey is fun.

6. She also called Grandpa Pappas.

7. Both of her grandfathers were glad to help with the family history.

8. Many of Sophie's friends had hobbies.

_____

_____

_____

_____

_____

_____

_____

_____

_____

_____

_____

_____

Using Time Order in Paragraphs

> ■ **Time order** is used to tell things in the order in which they happened. Some words that help show time order are <u>first</u>, <u>next</u>, <u>then</u>, <u>afterward</u>, and <u>finally</u>.

■ **Number the sentences below in the order in which the events happened. Place the topic sentence first. Then write the sentences in paragraph form. Remember to indent the first sentence.**

_____ **1.** He took a bus from Montréal to Toronto.

_____ **2.** He worked in Vancouver for three years.

_____ **3.** Casey came a long way on his journey to New Brunswick.

_____ **4.** First, he travelled by coach to Dublin, Ireland.

_____ **5.** Finally, he left Vancouver and drove all the way to Saint John.

_____ **6.** After working for five years in Toronto, he took a train to Vancouver.

_____ **7.** Then he took a ship from Dublin to Montréal.

_____ **8.** He lived in Montréal for two years.

_____ **9.** He stayed in Dublin for only two months.

_____ **10.** Now he enjoys telling about the cities he has lived in.

_____

_____

_____

_____

_____

_____

_____

_____

_____

_____

_____

Unit 5, Composition

Writing a Conversation

- When writing a **conversation**, be sure to:
  - Use quotation marks around each quote.
  - Use words such as <u>said</u> and <u>asked</u> with each quote.
  - Begin a new paragraph for each quote.
    - EXAMPLES: Sophie asked, "Will you tell me about your childhood?"
      Grandpa said, "Of course I will."

- **Rewrite the paragraph as a conversation between Sophie and Grandpa Pappas. Be sure to start a new paragraph for each quote.**

    Sophie asked Grandpa Pappas what it was like when he was growing up. Grandpa Pappas said he would tell her about his boyhood in Greece. He said that his father raised goats. He said that he used to watch the herd of goats for his father. Grandpa said it was not an easy job because wolves were always nearby. Sophie asked Grandpa Pappas to tell her about the wolves.

    Sophie asked, "What was it like when you were growing up?"

_____

_____

_____

_____

_____

_____

_____

_____

_____

_____

_____

_____

_____

- The **topic** is the subject you are writing about. The topic of a paragraph or story should be something that interests you.
- The **audience** is the person or people who will read what you wrote. Before starting to write, ask yourself some questions: Who will read this? How old are the people who will read this? What kinds of things are they interested in?

A. Next to the list of topics, write <u>adult</u>, <u>teenager</u>, or <u>child</u> to show who might be most interested in the topic.

_____   1.   A story about the amount of gas different car models use

_____   2.   A picture book about baby animals

_____   3.   A story about dirt-bike racing

_____   4.   A travel story about Spain

_____   5.   Nursery rhymes

_____   6.   A story about a rock group's travels

_____   7.   A story about teenage movie stars

_____   8.   Fairy tales

_____   9.   The life story of a famous writer for adults

_____   10.   A book of riddles

_____   11.   A book about home remodelling

B. Write five topics that are interesting. Then write the audience that you think might be interested in each topic.

Topic	Audience
1. _____	_____
2. _____	_____
3. _____	_____
4. _____	_____
5. _____	_____

- An **outline** is a plan to help organize writing. An outline lists the main ideas of a topic.
- An outline starts with a **statement** that tells the topic of the writing. The statement is followed by **main headings** and **subheadings** that tell what goes into each part. Main headings start with a roman numeral. Subheadings start with a capital letter.

Statement: Grandpa Pappas' life
(Main Heading)   II. Childhood
                         A. Born in Greece
(Subheadings)   B. Moved to Canada.
                    II. Adult Years
                         A. Worked in factory
                         B. Started grocery store

- **Choose one of your topics from page 76. Write an outline for that topic. Use the sample outline as a guide.**

Statement: _____

    I. _____

      A . _____

      B. _____

    II. _____

      A. _____

      B. _____

    III. _____

      A. _____

      B. _____

    IV. _____

      A. _____

      B. _____

A Narrative Paragraph

> ■ A **narrative paragraph** tells a story. A narrative paragraph usually tells events in the order in which they happened.

■ **Read the model paragraph. Then follow the directions.**

"Ah," said Grandpa, "my meeting with the wolf was very exciting. We had just arrived at the meadow. This day, the goats would not settle down. Athos, my dog, was acting strangely, too. He kept circling the goats, trying to keep them in a tight group. Suddenly, Athos leaped on the back of one goat and raced across the herd, back by back. Then, from a bunch of bushes, raced a huge grey form. 'Wolf!' my mind screamed, 'Wolf!' Athos reached the edge of the herd just as the wolf did. Without slowing down, Athos threw himself at the wolf. Next, I grabbed a stick and ran toward the wolf. I yelled and yelled and swung with the stick. I don't think I really ever touched the wolf. I was too scared to aim. Finally, I think he just got tired of all the noise we were making. He turned and trotted away. He didn't run, though. He made sure we knew that he wasn't afraid of us. Afterward, Athos and I were very proud of ourselves."

1. Underline the topic sentence, and circle the time order words.

2. List the events of the story in the proper time order and in your own words.

   1. They had just arrived at the meadow. _____

_____

_____

_____

_____

_____

_____

_____

_____

Writing a Narrative Paragraph

To write a narrative paragraph, follow these steps:
- Choose a topic, or subject.
- Decide who your audience will be.
- Write a topic sentence.
- Add supporting details.
- Use time order words to help the reader know when the events happened.

- **Choose a topic for a narrative paragraph. Write a topic sentence that will be the first sentence of your paragraph. Then add supporting sentences to complete the paragraph.**

Topic: _____

Topic Sentence: _____

_____

Paragraph:

_____

_____

_____

_____

_____

_____

_____

_____

_____

_____

_____

_____

_____

_____

_____

A. Write sentence if the group of words is a sentence. if the group of words is not a sentence, add what you need to make it a sentence. Then write the completed sentence on the line.

1. Sophie loved her grandfathers' stories.

   _____

2. Could listen for hours.

   _____

3. Their lives had been so exciting!

   _____

4. Wished her life was that interesting.

   _____

B. Read the paragraph. Underline the topic sentence.

> Sophie wanted to make a lasting history of her family. She took notes while her grandfathers spoke. They talked very fast, so she missed some things. She decided to record the stories on tape next time.

C. Write the topic sentence and supporting details in paragraph form. One sentence does not support the topic sentence. Do not include it in your paragraph.

Topic Sentence: Sophie planned her recorded history.

1. She read through her list of questions.
2. Then she thought about how much time each would take to answer.
3. Next, she went shopping for blank tapes.
4. She also found a new shirt she wanted to buy.
5. Finally, she was ready to let her grandfathers tell their stories.

   _____

   _____

   _____

   _____

   _____

D. Rewrite the paragraph as a conversation between Sophie and Grandpa Casey.

> Sophie asked Grandpa Casey how he came to Canada. Grandpa Casey told her of his trip from Ireland to Montréal by ship. Sophie asked him where his favourite place was. Grandpa Casey told her he liked it right where he was now.

_____

_____

_____

_____

E. Write the following as an outline on the lines provided.

Write a topic sentence	Write information about the topic
Choose a topic	Writing a narrative paragraph
Use time order words	Add supporting details

Statement: _____

      I. _____

     II. _____

    III. _____

        A. _____

        B. _____

F. Rewrite the sentences below in paragraph form. Write the topic sentence first. Circle the time order words.

1. Grandpa's twin brothers played tricks on people.
2. First, they'd dress exactly alike.
3. Then they'd both answer when people said one of their names.
4. Finally, they'd look at each other and laugh.

_____

_____

_____

_____

A. Choose a topic about an event.

Topic: _____

B. Try to limit your topic to one statement that explains it.

Statement: _____

_____

C. Write a short outline about your topic listing the major points you want to include. You might want to include the time, the place, the people involved, the actual event, any comments made about the event, and your feelings about the event.

I. _____

   A. _____

   B. _____

II. _____

   A. _____

   B. _____

III. _____

   A. _____

   B. _____

   C. _____

IV. _____

   A. _____

   B. _____

V. _____

   A. _____

   B. _____

   C. _____

D. Write a topic sentence about your topic.

Topic Sentence: _____

_____

E. Write a narrative paragraph. Begin with your topic sentence. Refer to your outline for supporting sentences. Remember to indent the first sentence.

_____

_____

_____

_____

_____

_____

_____

_____

_____

_____

_____

_____

_____

_____

_____

_____

_____

_____

_____

_____

Alphabetical Order

> - **Alphabetical order** is often used to organize names or words on a list. Use the first letter of each word to put the words in the order of the alphabet.
> - If two words begin with the same letter, look at the second letter to see which would come first.
>   EXAMPLE: **fan, fine**
> - If the first and second letters are the same, look at the third letter.
>   EXAMPLE: **fine, fire**

- **Read the groups of topics you have studied in this book. Number the terms in each group in alphabetical order.**

1. homonyms _____

synonyms _____

antonyms _____

suffixes _____

prefixes _____

contractions _____

vocabulary _____

opposites _____

2. index _____

accent _____

pronunciation _____

definitions _____

alphabetical _____

dictionaries _____

respellings _____

titles _____

copyright _____

3. statements _____

sentences _____

commands _____

subjects _____

predicates _____

exclamations _____

questions _____

run-ons _____

4. capitalization _____

punctuation _____

abbreviations _____

initials _____

quotes _____

commas _____

closing _____

greeting _____

periods _____

5. adjectives _____

nouns _____

verbs _____

adverbs _____

pronouns _____

apostrophes _____

possessives _____

tenses _____

6. topics _____

paragraphs _____

details _____

conversations _____

sentences _____

titles _____

narrative _____

audience _____

outlines _____

- **Guide words** are at the top of each page in a dictionary. Guide words tell the first and last words listed on each page. Every word listed on the page comes between the guide words.

  EXAMPLE: **million / modern**: The word <u>minute</u> will appear on the page. The word <u>music</u> will not.

A. Circle each word that would be on a page with these guide words.

1. alive / arrest	**2. flame/fourth**	**3. settle/sink**
anxious	fourth	side
amount	flower	shawl
accept	fog	seed
arrest	figure	seventeen
actor	fly	sink
alive	flame	service
also	fox	settle
adventure	flew	sign
ant	from	sleep
ashes	flight	shelter
allow	fruit	space

B. Rewrite each group of words in alphabetical order. Then write the words that would be the guide words for each group.

1. _____ / _____

lawn	_____
last	_____
lamp	_____
late	_____
lap	_____
lake	_____
lead	_____

2. _____ / _____

palm	_____
page	_____
pass	_____
pad	_____
pack	_____
pan	_____
pat	_____

Dictionary Pronunciation

- Each word listed in a dictionary is followed by a respelling of the word. The respelling shows how to **pronounce**, or say, the word. The respelling is in parentheses following the entry word.
- **Accent marks** show which word parts are said with the most force.   EXAMPLE: freedom (frē´ dəm)   beauty (byü´ tē)
- A **pronunciation key** (shown below) contains letters and special symbols, along with sample words, that show how the letters should be pronounced.

A. Write the word from the box for each respelling. Use the pronunciation key on the right.

gallop	hug	trout
girl	huge	vanish
glide	lowly	write

hat, āge, fär; let, ēqual, tėrm; it, īce; hot, ōpen, ôrder; oil, out; cup, put, rüle; əbove, takən, pencəl, lemən, circəs; ch, child; ng, long; sh, ship; th, thin; ŦH, then; zh, measure

1. (gėrl) _____

2. (lō´ lē) _____

3. (rīt) _____

4. (trout) _____

5. (glīd) _____

6. (hyü) _____

7. (gal´ əp) _____

8. (hug) _____

9. (van´ ish) _____

B. Complete each sentence. Write the word in the blank next to its respelling.

dictionary	found	guide	respelling	word

1. David didn't know how to say the (wėrd) _____ protection.

2. He took out his (dik´ shə ner´ ē) _____ .

3. He used (gīd) _____ words to find the page.

4. Then he (found) _____ the word.

5. The (rē spel´ ing) _____ was listed right after the word.

    He practised saying it correctly.

                    Unit 6, Study Skills

> - The **definition**, or meaning, is given for each word listed in a dictionary. Sometimes a definition is followed by a sentence showing a use for the word.
> - The **parts of speech** are also given for each word.
>   EXAMPLE: **glove** (gluv) *n.* a covering for the hand: *I found a red glove on the bench at the park.*

A. Use the dictionary entries below to answer the questions.

folk tale (fōk´ tāl´) *n.* a story or legend originating, as a rule, among the people of a region or country and handed down from generation to generation.
fol·low·er (fol´ ō ər) *n.* **1** a person or thing that follows. **2** a person who follows the ideas or beliefs of another: *Buddhists are followers of Buddha.*
fol·ly (fol´ ē) *n.* **1** being foolish; lack of sense; unwise conduct. **2** a foolish act, practice, or idea; something silly.
fond (fond) *adj.* **1** loving; liking: *a fond look.*
for·bid (fər bid´) *v.* order one not to do something; make a rule against; prohibit.

n.	noun
pron.	pronoun
v.	verb
adj.	adjective
adv.	adverb
prep.	preposition

1. What part of speech is <u>folk tale</u>? _____

2. What does <u>adj.</u> following the respelling of <u>fond</u> stand for? _____

3. What does <u>v.</u> following the respelling of <u>forbid</u> stand for? _____

4. Which words in the dictionary sample are nouns? _____

5. Write a sentence for the word <u>folly</u>. _____

_____

B. Use a dictionary to look up the meaning of each of the words below. Write a sentence for each word.

1. griddle _____

_____

2. injury _____

_____

3. landlord _____

_____

4. pleasing _____

_____

> ■ Some words have more than one meaning, or **multiple meanings**. In the dictionary, the meanings for these words are numbered.
>
> EXAMPLE: **hard** (härd) *adj.* **1** very firm. **2** difficult: *The letter was hard to read.*

A. Use the dictionary entries below to answer the questions.

bar·ri·er (bar´ ē ər *or* ber´ē ər) *n.* **1** something that stands in the way: *A dam is a barrier holding water back.* **2** something stopping progress or preventing approach: *Lack of water was a barrier to the settlement of that region.* **3** something that separates or keeps apart: *The Atlantic Ocean is a barrier between the British Isles and Canada.*
beam (bēm) *n.* **1** a large, long piece of timber, ready for use in building. **2** ray or rays of light or heat: *the beam from a flashlight* **3** a bright look or smile.
bold (bōld) *adj.* **1** without fear; daring: *a bold knight, a bold explorer.* **2** too free in manner; impudent: *The bold little girl made faces at us.* **3** striking; vigorous; free; clear: *The mountains stood in bold outline against the sky.*
bor·row (bô´ rō) *v.* **1** get something from another person with the understanding that it must be returned. **2** take and use as one's own; adopt; take: *Rome borrowed many ideas from Greece.*
by (bī) *prep.* **1** near; beside: *The garden is by the house.* **2** along; over; through: *to go by the bridge.* **3** through the action of: *The thief was captured by a police officer.* **4** through the means or use of: *They keep in touch by letter.* **5** not later than: *We'll try to be there by six o'clock.*

n.	noun
pron.	pronoun
v.	verb
adj.	adjective
adv.	adverb
prep.	preposition

1. How many definitions are listed for the word <u>barrier</u>? _____ for the word <u>beam</u>? _____ for the word <u>bold</u>? _____

2. How many definitions are given for the word <u>borrow</u>? _____ for the word <u>by</u>? _____

B. Write the number of the dictionary definition for the underlined word.

_____ 1. A <u>barrier</u> kept the fans off the playing field.

_____ 2. The mayor <u>borrowed</u> a joke from a friend to use in a speech.

_____ 3. Wooden <u>beams</u> were used to build the barn.

_____ 4. The <u>bold</u> captain guided the ship through the storm.

_____ 5. They drove <u>by</u> the park, on the way home.

Using an Encyclopedia

- An **encyclopedia** is a reference book that has articles on many different subjects. The articles are arranged in alphabetical order in different books, called **volumes**. Each volume is marked to show which subjects are inside.
- **Guide words** are used to show the first subject on each page.
- There is a listing of **cross-references** at the end of most articles to related subjects that the reader can use to get more information on that subject.

A. Read the sample encyclopedia entry below. Use it to answer the questions that follow.

VITAMINS are an important part of health. They cannot be produced by the body. Vitamins must be included in the diet. It is important to eat a variety of foods so your body will get all the vitamins it needs to stay healthy. Vitamins may be needed in increased amounts during periods of rapid growth, during stress, and while recovering from an illness. See also MINERALS.

1. What is the article about? _____

2. Why are vitamins important? _____

3. Why should you eat a variety of foods? _____

4. When might more vitamins be needed? _____

5. What other subject could you look at to get more information? _____

MINERALS are elements that serve as building blocks or take part in chemical processes in the body. Most of the mineral content of the body is in the bones. Calcium is an important mineral that aids in the formation of teeth and bones, blood clotting, and the activity of muscles and nerves. Minerals are found in foods.

6. Why do you think this cross-reference is included in the article about vitamins?

_____

7. Does the above cross-reference mention vitamins? _____

> ■ When looking for an article in the encyclopedia:
> Always look up the last name of a person.
>   EXAMPLE: To find an article on Babe Ruth, look under Ruth.
>   Look up the first word in the name of a place.
>   EXAMPLE: To find an article on New Brunswick, look under New.
> Look up the most important word in the name of a general topic.
>   EXAMPLE: To find an article on the brown bear, look under bear.

B. Write the word you would look under to find an article on each of the following subjects.

1. Nelson Mandela _____

2. frozen food _____

3. United States _____

4. oceans of the world _____

5. Margaret Thatcher _____

6. United Kingdom _____

7. children's games _____

8. breeds of dogs _____

C. The example below shows how the volumes of one encyclopedia are marked. The subjects are in alphabetical order. Write the number of the volume in which you would find each article.

A	B	C-CH	CI-CZ	D	E	F	G	H	I-J	K	L
1	2	3	4	5	6	7	8	9	10	11	12

M	N	O	P	Q-R	S	T	U-V	W-X-Y-Z	INDEX
13	14	15	16	17	18	19	20	21	22

_____ 1. caring for horses   _____ 5. mammals

_____ 2. life stages of the butterfly   _____ 6. Buckingham Palace

_____ 3. making paper   _____ 7. yeast

_____ 4. underwater plants   _____ 8. coniferous trees

Parts of a Book

- The **title page** tells the name of a book and usually the name of its author.
- The **copyright page** tells who published the book, where it was published, and when it was published.
- The **table of contents** lists the chapter or unit titles and the page numbers on which they begin. It is at the front of a book.
- The **index** gives a detailed list of the topics in a book. It gives the page numbers for each topic. It is at the back of a book.

■ **Use this book to answer the questions.**

1. What is the title of this book?

   _____

2. On what page does Unit Three start? _____

3. List the pages that deal with apostrophes. _____

4. What is the copyright date of this book? _____

5. On what page is the lesson on prefixes?

   _____

6. On what page does Unit Six start? _____

7. On what page is the index? _____

8. List the pages that deal with adverbs. _____

9. What lesson is on page 42? _____

10. On what pages are the lessons on action verbs? _____

11. What company published this book?

    _____

12. What lesson is on page 79?

    _____

A. Write the following words in alphabetical order.

fruit   onion

morning   wag

pizza   ran

1. _____   4. _____

2. _____   5. _____

3. _____   6. _____

B. Write the words in alphabetical order under the correct guide words.

1. **dear / delicious**   2. **delight / develop**

_____   _____

_____   _____

_____   _____

_____   _____

depend
degree
debt
den
defend
demand
design
deck

C. Complete each sentence. Write the word in the blank next to its respelling.

1. If you (nēd) _____ help with a word, look in the dictionary.

2. The (dik´ shə ner´ ē) _____ tells you what a word means.

3. It also tells you how to (sā) _____ the word.

4. Often the word is used in a (sen´ təns) _____ .

dictionary
need
say
sentence

D. Use the dictionary entries below to answer the questions.

chuck (chuk) *v.* **1** pat; tap, especially under the chin. **2** throw; toss. **3** *Informal.* give up or finish with: *He's chucked his job.*
ours (ourz *or* ärz) *pron.* a possessive of **we**: that which belongs to us: *That car is ours.*

1. What part of speech is the entry word <u>chuck</u>? _____

2. Which word is a pronoun? _____

3. Which word has more than one meaning? _____

n.	noun
pron.	pronoun
v.	verb
adj.	adjective
adv.	adverb
prep.	preposition

E. Use the sample encyclopedia entry to answer the questions.

> **GREY OWL** (1888–1938) was born in England of English parents, but passed himself off as an Apache for most of his life. He moved to Canada when he was 17. As Grey Owl, he wrote and lectured on the need to preserve the wilderness. People did not discover his true identity until after his death. See also BELANEY, ARCHIBALD S.

1. Who is the article about?_____

2. Where was he born?_____

3. When did he come to Canada?_____

4. What did he write about?_____

5. Why do you think the cross-reference is Archibald S. Belaney?_____

_____

F. The example below shows how the volumes of an encyclopedia are marked. Circle the word you would look under to find an article on each of the following. Then write the number of the volume in which you would find each article.

A–C	D–F	G–H	I–L	M–N	O–R	S–T	U–W	X–Z
1	2	3	4	5	6	7	8	9

_____ 1. the history of computers   _____ 4. animals of Norway

_____ 2. Albert Einstein   _____ 5. the capital of Romania

_____ 3. the Amazon River   _____ 6. bald eagles

G. Write title page, copyright page, table of contents, or index to tell where you would find this information.

1. The author's name _____

2. The title of the book _____

3. The page on which particular information can be found _____

4. The year the book was published _____

5. The page on which a certain chapter starts _____

6. The company that published the book _____

A. Use a social studies book to complete the exercise.

1. Find the title on the title page of the book.

    Write the title. _____

2. Find the name of the publisher and the year it
    was published.

    Write this information. _____

3. Find the names of the authors.

    Write the names. _____

4. How many sections or chapters are there in the book?

    Write the number. _____

5. Look carefully at the index.

    How are the words in the index listed? _____

6. Choose a topic you have already studied this year
    in class.

    Write the topic. _____

7. Look in the index for page numbers on which information
    about this topic can be found.

    Write the page numbers. _____

8. In what chapter or chapters does the information
    about this person appear?

    Write the chapter numbers. _____

**B. Look up the word happiness in a dictionary. Then follow the directions
below.**

1. Tell what part of speech happiness is. _____

2. Copy the first definition. _____

3. Write a sentence using the word happiness. _____

    _____

4. Copy the respelling. _____

C. Rewrite the words in alphabetical order. Then find the words in a dictionary. Next to each word, write the guide words from the top of the page and the respelling of the word.

| blizzard | scent | magician | howl | venture |
| helpful | remind | ache | ancient | disease |

	Words	**Guide Words**	**Respelling**
1.	ache	accuse/acorn	āk
2.			
3.			
4.			
5.			
6.			
7.			
8.			
9.			
10.			

D. Find the entry for <u>Laura Second</u> in a Canadian encyclopedia. Then answer the following questions.

1. What encyclopedia did you use? _____

2. When did Laura Secord live? _____

3. Where did she die? _____

4. Why is Laura Secord famous? _____

_____

5. Whose plans did she overhear? _____

Synonyms ■ **Find the pair of synonyms in each sentence. Write each pair on the lines.**

1. Ruth smiled at Lea, and her friend grinned back.

   _____   _____

2. He ran out the door and dashed down the street.

   _____   _____

3. She spoke with Sarah, and then talked to her boss.

   _____   _____

Antonyms ■ **For each underlined word, circle the correct antonym at the end of the sentence.**

1. He tried to find the <u>correct</u> answer.   (write, wrong)
2. She <u>forgot</u> to pick up her clothes at the cleaners.   (refused, remembered)
3. Mico was <u>happy</u> to join the team.   (pleased, sad)

Homonyms ■ **Circle the correct homonym to complete each sentence.**

1. Joe and Jane did not (hear, here) the alarm.
2. They were (to, too, two) busy to notice it.
3. (Its, It's) hard to believe that, since the alarm is so loud.
4. I guess (there, their, they're) used to loud noises.
5. They were surprised to see (to, too, two) men run (right, write) past them.
6. The police got (there, their, they're) quickly.
7. They asked Joe and Jane to (right, write) down what they saw.
8. The police said about the alarm, "(Its, It's) purpose (hear, here) is to warn people."
9. Joe and Jane hung (there, their, they're) heads.
10. They were (to, too, two) embarrassed (to, too, two) say anything.

Multiple Meanings ■ **Circle the correct meaning for each underlined word.**

1. Hank grabbed a rock to <u>arm</u> himself against the stray dog.

   part of the body   take up a weapon

2. The angry <u>bark</u> scared him.

   noise a dog makes   outside a covering on a tree

3. Hank made a <u>dash</u> for safety.

   a dotted line   a run

Prefixes and Suffixes ■ Write <u>P</u> if the underlined word has a prefix. Write <u>S</u> if it has a suffix.

_____ **1.** The thieves <u>disappeared</u>.

_____ **2.** One <u>rethought</u> what he had done.

_____ **3.** The <u>harmless</u> prank had gone wrong.

_____ **4.** He was <u>doubtful</u> anyone would understand.

_____ **5.** They could not <u>undo</u> what they had done.

Compound Words ■ Underline the compound word in each sentence. Then write the two words that form each compound word on the lines.

1. My favourite dessert is strawberries and ice cream.

_____   _____

2. One of the most dangerous snakes is the rattlesnake.

_____   _____

3. He will use sandpaper to smooth the rough wood.

_____   _____

Contractions ■ Write the contraction for each pair of words.

1. it is _____

2. could not _____

3. they will _____

4. I am _____

5. will not _____

Compound Words and Contractions ■ Circle each compound word, and underline each contraction in the paragraph.

Many people think she's gone to the seashore. But they're wrong. She'd rather go to her mountaintop hideaway. She'll stay there until somebody gets worried. Then they'll remember and call her there. She won't let anything but an emergency make her come back until she's ready!

Recognizing Sentences ▪ Write <u>S</u> if the group of words is a sentence.
Write <u>X</u> if the group of words is not a sentence.

_____ 1. Do you need?

_____ 2. Something from the store.

_____ 3. I need milk and bread.

_____ 4. I'll get them for you.

_____ 5. If only.

_____ 6. Will you go before noon?

_____ 7. Then we can make lunch.

_____ 8. Before Ellen and Jim return.

Types of Sentences ▪ Write <u>declarative</u>, <u>interrogative</u>, <u>imperative</u>, or <u>exclamatory</u>
to show what type each sentence is.

_____ 1. Do you have a ticket to the game?

_____ 2. No, I left mine at home!

_____ 3. Buy a new one.

_____ 4. Tickets cost three dollars.

_____ 5. Isn't it worth it?

_____ 6. Yes, I just don't have any money with me.

_____ 7. I will buy one for you.

_____ 8. Okay, let's go!

Subjects and Predicates ▪ Write <u>subject</u> or <u>predicate</u> to show which part of each
sentence is underlined.

_____ 1. Deserts <u>receive the least amount of rainfall of any region</u>.

_____ 2. <u>Deserts</u> have little or no plant life.

_____ 3. Some deserts <u>are found near the equator</u>.

_____ 4. <u>Many desert regions</u> have hot summers and cold winters.

Simple Subjects and Predicates ▪ Circle the simple subject, and underline the simple
predicate in each sentence.

1. For years factories dumped wastes into lakes and rivers.

2. Some waste materials caused no harm.

3. Other waste poisoned the water.

4. Today many factories protect the water from wastes.

Simple and Compound Sentences ■ Write <u>simple</u> or <u>compound</u> before each sentence.

_____ 1. We know about all nine planets in our solar system, but we know most about Earth.

_____ 2. Earth travels around the sun.

_____ 3. Each planet follows a different path around the sun.

_____ 4. It takes about 365 days for Earth to travel around the sun, and we call this period of time one year.

_____ 5. Earth spins as it goes around the sun.

_____ 6. This spin lets the sun shine on different parts of Earth at different times, and this causes day and night.

Combining Sentences ■ Combine each pair of simple sentences into a compound sentence.

1. Jessie went fishing. Ted went swimming.

_____

2. Yesterday was cold. Today is a rainy, grey day.

_____

3. Canada and the United States are neighbours. Canada and the United States are friends.

_____

Run-on Sentences ■ Rewrite the story by separating each run-on sentence.

Few people know that Canada had its own pirate, his name was Peter Easton. He arrived in Newfoundland in 1610, he built a fort at Harbour Grace. Many a fishing fleet was looted by his pirate crew. Once, though, Easton defended Harbour Grace against an attack by Basques, for that he was pardoned, the end of his life was spent in luxury as the Marquis of Savoy.

_____

_____

_____

_____

_____

_____

Nouns—Proper and Common ▪ Circle the common nouns, and underline the proper nouns.

1. Sally sat next to the window.

2. It was a wonderful morning in June.

3. Summer days in Halifax are very beautiful.

Nouns—Singular, Plural, and Possessive ▪ Circle the correct form of each noun.

1. Our female (dog, dog's) puppies are brown and white.

2. All the (puppy's, puppies') ears are long.

3. Our other (dogs, dog's) stay away from the puppies.

4. The puppies' (tail's, tails) wag all the time.

Verbs—Action, Linking, and Helping ▪ Write A, L, or H to tell if the underlined verb is an action, linking, or helping verb.

_____ 1. The storm blew in quickly.

_____ 2. We felt the weather change.

_____ 3. We are going back to the house.

_____ 4. Then lightning split the sky.

_____ 5. Rain was predicted.

_____ 6. The storm is very strong.

Verb Tenses ▪ Write past, present, or future for each underlined verb.

_____ 1. Most hurricanes form in the spring.

_____ 2. We hope the next hurricane will not hit the coast.

_____ 3. The last hurricane slammed into Cuba.

Verbs—Making Subjects and Verbs Agree ▪ Circle the verb in each sentence. Then write singular or plural to show the number of the subject and verb.

_____ 1. There are people who check facts for a living.

_____ 2. They read articles to be sure the truth is told.

_____ 3. Henry is one of those people.

_____ 4. He likes his job very much.

Pronouns ■ Rewrite each sentence using the correct pronoun for the underlined noun. Then label each pronoun, using <u>S</u> for subject, <u>O</u> for object, or <u>P</u> for possessive.

_____ 1. <u>Carol's</u> job is park ranger.

_____

_____ 2. <u>Carol</u> loves spending every day in the forest.

_____

_____ 3. Her favourite thing is walking among <u>the trees</u>.

_____

_____ 4. She really likes it when <u>the trees'</u> leaves change.

_____

_____ 5. Ed sometimes brings <u>Ed's</u> camera to take pictures.

_____

_____ 6. <u>The camera's</u> pictures are clear and sharp.

_____

Adjectives and Adverbs ■ Write adjective or adverb for each underlined word.

_____ 1. Sachiko walked <u>slowly</u> into the room.

_____ 2. Her <u>bright</u> jacket seemed out of place.

_____ 3. Her <u>shaky</u> voice showed how scared she was.

_____ 4. Her eyes looked <u>larger</u> than normal.

_____ 5. <u>Soon</u> she began to calm down.

_____ 6. <u>Finally</u>, she spoke with confidence.

Using Words Correctly ■ Circle the correct word to complete each sentence.

1. I (doesn't, don't) want to be late for the meeting.
2. Nobody (never, ever) remembers exactly what happened.
3. I like to take (good, well) notes.
4. Then I can review (those, them) later.
5. It (doesn't, don't) take long to get there.
6. I just need to find (them, those) directions.
7. Everything will turn out (good, well).

Capitalization and Punctuation ▪ Rewrite the letter below. Add capital letters, periods, commas, question marks, and quotation marks where needed.

328 brant st s

north york on m2c 4g1

january 2 1997

dear dr turner

   I want to thank you for your kindness to tootsie my pet

bird my friend Jack said, no one knows how to cure birds they're

different from other types of pets you shouldn't

waste your money can you believe that I didn't agree with Jack

so I brought tootsie to your office thanks to you,

tootsie is fine again

sincerely

philip chow

Capitalization and Punctuation ▪ Rewrite each sentence correctly.

1. our next topic said mr lopez will be the fall of the roman empire

_____

2. hurry and get out of there cried louis

_____

3. ted please don't ask me to do that

_____

4. has the jury reached a verdict asked judge mallory

_____

5. eric said i'll be the first to tell you if you're right

_____

6. well i guess it's all right

_____

7. we spent the day swimming hiking and having a picnic

_____

Using Apostrophes ▪ Rewrite the sentences. Insert apostrophes where they are needed.

1. Didnt you see the look on Deans face?

_____

2. Its pretty clear he doesnt like our plan.

_____

3. He hasnt said anything at all about Francos idea.

_____

4. Were going to have to make up our minds soon.

_____

5. The mens ideas are different from ours.

_____

6. Everyones ideas should be considered.

_____

Topic Sentences and Supporting Details ■ Underline the topic sentence. Draw a line through details that do not support the topic sentence. Then circle the time order words. Rewrite the remaining sentences on the lines below.

Forests grow in a cycle. There are many kinds of animals in a forest. First, the strongest trees grow very large. Then the other trees cannot get enough sunlight. Weaker trees either stay short or die. Afterward, new growth begins. Sometimes fires destroy a whole forest.

_____

_____

_____

_____

_____

Writing a Conversation ■ Rewrite the paragraph as a conversation between Chris and Bob.

Bob asked Chris if he understood the movie. Chris said he wasn't sure. He thought he had at first, but then he became confused. Bob agreed. Chris asked Bob what he thought about the movie. Bob said he liked it, but he wondered about the ending. Chris said the person who wrote it was probably as confused as they were!

_____

_____

_____

_____

_____

_____

_____

 Composition

Planning an Outline ■ Write the following as an outline on the lines provided.

Mammals

Wombats

Animals of Australia

Marsupials

Kangaroos

Statement: _____

      I. _____

         A. _____

         B. _____

     II. _____

A Narrative Paragraph ■ Rewrite the paragraph in the correct order.

    Judy had planned her day well. After that, she went shopping for a special meal. Tonight she would invite her parents over for dinner. Then she bought a beautiful bunch of flowers. First, she cleaned her entire house. She chose the clothes she would wear. Next, she went to the florist and bought a blue glass vase. She took the vase and flowers back home and put them on the table. Finally, she prepared the meal and waited for her parents to arrive.

_____

_____

_____

_____

_____

_____

_____

_____

_____

_____

_____

Alphabetical Order and Guide Words ▪ Rewrite each list in alphabetical order. Then write the words that would be the guide words for each list.

Guide Words

_____ / _____

1. right _____
2. rock _____
3. rich _____
4. rinse _____
5. rob _____

Guide Words

_____ / _____

1. bat _____
2. back _____
3. ball _____
4. base _____
5. baby _____

Pronunciation ▪ Use a dictionary to find each word listed. Write the respelling of each word.

1. now _____
2. later _____
3. tomorrow _____

4. today _____
5. direct _____
6. scissors _____

Dictionary Definitions ▪ Use the dictionary entry below to answer the questions.

bet·ter (bet´ər) *adj.* **1** more desirable, useful, etc. than another: *a better plan*. **2** of superior quality: *better bread*. **3** less sick: *The child is better today*. *–v.* **1** make or become better; improve: *We can better our work by being careful*. **2** do better than; surpass: *The other class cannot better our grades*.

n.	noun
pron.	pronoun
v.	verb
adj.	adjective
adv.	adverb
prep.	preposition

1. What does <u>adj.</u> stand for? _____

2. How many definitions for <u>better</u> are given?_____

3. What two parts of speech can <u>better</u> be?_____

4. Which part of speech and definition number are used for <u>better</u> in these sentences?

   a. She has bettered her tennis form._____

   b. That horse is the better cow pony._____

   c. He has a better car than his father has._____

106 **Study Skills**

Using an Encyclopedia ■ **Read the sample encyclopedia entry below. Use it to answer the questions that follow.**

> **ELBOW** The elbow is a joint between the upper and lower arm. This joint allows the arm to bend, twist, and turn. Groups of muscles and tendons make the elbow work. One of the best tools the body has is the arm. It allows a person to reach out, hold, and control things. *See also* ARM *and* WRIST.

1. What is the article about? _____

2. What is the elbow? _____

3. Why is the elbow important? _____

4. What are the cross-references? _____

5. Are both cross-references mentioned in the article? _____

Using an Encyclopedia ■ **Circle the word you would look under to find an article on each of the following. Then write the number of the volume in which you would find it.**

A–C	D–F	G–I	J–L	M–N	O–Q	R–S	T–V	W–Z
1	2	3	4	5	6	7	8	9

_____ 1. the sea floor

_____ 2. Hong Kong

_____ 3. nursing skills

_____ 4. the life cycle of the fly

_____ 5. Anne Frank

_____ 6. how aluminum is made

_____ 7. the truth about vampires

_____ 8. breeds of horses

_____ 9. the plays of Shakespeare

_____ 10. boomerangs as weapons

_____ 11. string instruments

_____ 12. New Orleans

Parts of a Book ■ **Write <u>title page</u>, <u>copyright page</u>, <u>table of contents</u>, or <u>index</u> to tell where you would find this information.**

1. a chapter title _____

2. the page on which certain information can be found _____

3. the author's name _____

4. the year the book was published _____

Index